FAITH, SCIENCE AND UNDERSTANDING

Faith,
Science and
Understanding

JOHN POLKINGHORNE

Yale University Press   New Haven and London

Published 2000 in the United States by Yale University Press and
in Great Britain by SPCK Publishing.

Set in Janson type by Tseng Information Systems, Durham, North
Carolina.

Printed in the United States of America.

Library of Congress Cataloging-in-Publication Data
Polkinghorne, J. C., 1930–
Faith, science and understanding / John Polkinghorne.
p. cm.
Includes bibliographical references and index.
ISBN 0-300-08372-6 (alk. paper)
1. Religion and science. I. Title.
BL241 .P563 2000
261.5′5—dc21   00-026934

A catalogue record for this book is available from the British Library.

The paper in this book meets the guidelines for permanence and durability
of the Committee on Production Guidelines for Book Longevity of the
Council on Library Resources.

10 9 8 7 6 5 4 3 2 1

To

the Clergy and People
of the Parish of the Good Shepherd,
Cambridge

fides quaerens intellectum
faith seeking understanding

—St Anselm

Contents

Preface

After I had written a trilogy of short books about science and theology, I permitted myself the liberty of writing a subsequent volume, *Reason and Reality*, that enabled me to return to some of the issues then raised in somewhat greater depth. Since then I have written four books that each, in their own particular way, seek to contribute to the presently burgeoning field of science and theology studies: my Gifford Lectures, *Science and Christian Belief* (in the United States, *The Faith of a Physicist*); a survey of the writings of scientist-theologians, *Scientists as Theologians*; my Terry Lectures, *Belief in God in an Age of Science;* and an introductory textbook, *Science and Theology*. I now wish to offer a second 'further thoughts' volume, looking again at some of the issues raised in these four books.

The first section of the book is concerned with a number of key issues that arise in the interaction between science and theology. Its underlying basis is the conviction that both disciplines have things of value to say to each other because both, in their differing domains of experience, are concerned with the search for truth attained by the formation and evaluation of motivated beliefs.

The invitation to give the Firth Lectures at the University of Nottingham gave me the opportunity to reflect on the place of theology in the university. What I said then is the basis for the first two chapters of this book. In chapter 1, I defend the concepts of the value of knowledge for knowledge's sake and of the essential unity of knowledge. I believe these to be the foundations on which the life of a university is built. If theology does not make its own distinctive contribution to this intellectual endeavour, the enterprise of higher education is incomplete. In the course of an open search for understanding, the personal and subjective elements of human experience must be accorded equal weight with the impersonal and objective aspects which constitute science's self-limited domain of enquiry. In chapter 2, I draw upon science's success in its own task, to give encouragement both to the due recognition of an inescapable degree of precariousness present in all forms of human search for knowledge, and also to resist succumbing to epistemological despair. Theology's appeal to revelation is seen as being recourse to illuminating experience, analogous to science's recourse to observation and experiment, and not an appeal to some ineffable and unquestionable authority.

In chapter 3, I further look at the role of revelation in religion, so often felt by enquiring scientists to constitute a stumbling block for them. The particular and unique has a necessary significance in the realm of the personal and transpersonal. Scripture is the record of remarkable individual encounters with the divine, but it is neither uniform in its character nor immune from critical evaluation. It is to be read as evidence for the way in which God has made the divine nature known, and not as a textbook in which God has provided ready-made answers for our unquestioning acceptance.

Among contemporary scientists, biologists tend to be much more sceptical of religion, and indeed often hostile to it, than are many physicists. Therefore, it was an unexpected development in the 1990s to see some revival of the discussion of teleological arguments among certain biologists. Chapter 4 gives a concise survey of this activity and an assessment of its possible relevance to theology. Questions of significant interest have certainly been raised, but a cautious view is taken of what metaphysical conclusions might flow from this.

In chapter 5, five short essays are gathered together that reconsider topics that have received considerable recent attention in the interaction between science and theology. First, critical realism is defended in the face of the apparent discontinuity involved in moving from Newton's inverse square law of gravitation to Einstein's geometry of curved space. The conclusion is that it is only at the level of the fundamental mathematical structures, that underlie physically picturable models, that the degree of continuity of account that realism demands is to be discerned. This recognition reinforces the perception of mathematics as being the fundamental language of physical science. Second, attempts to use quantum cosmology as a device for generating a many-worlds interpretation of anthropic coincidences are shown to be no more than somewhat desperate metaphysical strategies. Third, panentheism is looked at again in the light of a vigorous defence of that concept mounted recently by Philip Clayton. I remain unconvinced, presenting some critiques of Clayton's arguments. In my opinion it remains unclear why one should not be content simply to achieve a balance between divine transcendence and divine immanence without recourse to doubtful panentheistic language. Fourth, a form of dual-aspect monism is reconsidered in which the material and the mental are complementary to each other. It is supposed that the truths of mathematics are entities existing at the extreme mental pole (just as stones exist at the extreme material pole). This leads to the conclusion that the duality involved is not only mental/material but also being/becoming and everlasting/temporal. Finally, I try yet again to correct certain persistent misunderstandings about my proposals for an ontologically realistic interpretation of chaos theory.

Part 2 of the book is concerned with what was the dominant issue in the science and theology debate in the 1990s: How we may conceive of divine agency in a way that respects the integrity of the scientific account of the process of the physical world and which also does justice to the religious intuition and experience of God's providential interaction within history?

Chapter 6 provides an overview of the issues. There are two novel features in the discussion here presented. One is the employment of a typology of attitudes to nature, first presented by the historian of ideas R. G. Collingwood. The other is a putting into question the traditional theological assumption that God should never be considered as acting as a cause among causes. I suggest that divine self-limitation, implied in the act of allowing the being of the creaturely other, can be held to extend to the divine condescension involved in providential action functioning as a cause among the causes of the world. A key theological concept in this discussion is the idea that the act of creation was an act of divine kenosis, a voluntary limitation accepted by God as the necessary consequence of the divine love allowing the creation truly to be itself.

In chapter 7, I discuss the nature of time as a means of exploring how one might propose different chains of alogical linkings together of scientific, metaphysical and theological ideas, in certain clusters of natural association. This chapter makes the greatest technical demands upon the reader, though I have reduced these demands to the minimum that is compatible with a careful treatment of the issues. Because science does not determine metascience, though it certainly constrains it, several different schemes are explored and evaluated in the chapter.

Part 3 concentrates on the contributions that a variety of significant thinkers have made to the interaction between science and theology.

In *Scientists as Theologians* I discussed the work of three contemporary scientist-theologians. In chapter 8, I extend this survey by considering the work of two theologians, Wolfhart Pannenberg and Thomas Torrance, who have taken a serious interest in scientific matters, and the work of a scientist, Paul Davies, who, though standing outside any religious tradition, has nevertheless shown considerable interest in the possibilities of theistic explanation.

Discussing the relationship between science and theology has been a preoccupation of the English. My final chapter reviews this long history, stretching over several centuries, finding it to be anchored in a national tendency to move from experience to understanding, of a kind that I have labelled 'bottom-up thinking'.

Acknowledgements

Chapters 1 and 2 are based on my Firth Lectures given at Nottingham University in 1997, and chapter 6 on my Witherspoon Lecture given at the Center of Theological Inquiry at Princeton in 1998, which also appeared in *Reflections* (Center of Theological Inquiry, 1999). Chapter 9 is a modified version of a lecture I gave at a Conference in Heidelberg in 1998, organised by Professor Michael Welker. In each case I am grateful for a kind invitation and generous hospitality. Chapter 7 is based on a paper published in *Theology Today* (55, 329–343, 1998) and the material of 8.1 is a considerably expanded version of a paper published in *Zygon* (34, 151–158, 1999). I am grateful to the respective Editors for their permission to reuse this material.

I am also grateful to the staff of Yale University Press for assistance in preparing the manuscript for press, and to my wife, Ruth, for help in correcting the proofs.

Part I

ISSUES

CHAPTER ONE

Theology in the University

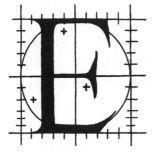 VER since their origins in the late Middle Ages, universities have been sources of trained personnel apt for the service of the community, whether by providing clerks for the Royal Court or canon lawyers for the service of the Church. Advances in scientific technology, which have done so much to define the context of our life today, have only broadened and intensified the importance of this role. I believe that the universities can claim significant success in meeting this need. It would, however, be a bad error to mistake a valuable byproduct for the principal object of activity. The essential purpose of a regime of physical exercise and good nutrition is the maintenance of health. If it also produces some excellent football players, that is to be welcomed, but that result is a collateral good rather than the main objective. The essential purpose of a university is the discovery and propagation of knowledge. Many other goods will derive from the fulfilment of that main objective, but their

continuance depends, in the long run, upon not losing sight of the central aim. I state very clearly my belief in the value of knowledge for knowledge's sake, together with my belief in the essential unity of all knowledge. Universities are the institutionalised expressions of these beliefs.

I became very aware of these issues in the late 1970s when I was briefly Chairman of the Nuclear Physics Board of what was then called the Science Research Council (SRC). It was my job to ask the British taxpayer, through SRC, for the £40 million or so necessary to finance our national contribution to the international field of research into the fundamental structure of matter. Then, as always, money was short and the arguments between the different sciences seeking their share of what was available, correspondingly intense. We particle physicists were studying the behaviour of matter in extreme regimes that were far removed from circumstances relevant to everyday technology. In fact, that was the source of much of the expense, since such unusual states of matter could be created only in accelerators costing hundreds of millions of pounds to build and tens of millions of pounds per year to run. These machines were too expensive for any single European nation to construct and maintain on their own, but we belonged to CERN, the international consortium that ran this activity in Europe. Developing precision engineering on kilometre scales, and control devices with nanosecond response times, certainly generated remarkable technical advances that would find application outside the particle physicists' specialised field of use. Many talented young people served their scientific apprenticeship within our community, and most of them subsequently went on to use the skills they had acquired in a variety of totally different contexts. In terms of spin-off, there was much that could be said for particle physics. But when the chips were finally down, when the last round of argument was in progress about whether it was to be £40 million or only 35, there was just one central honest argument to be used in our cause. It was that to understand the fundamental structure of the matter of the universe, to unravel the mysteries of quarks and gluons, was in itself a worthwhile thing to do, a high human achievement that did not need to find its justification outside itself. It was a case of knowledge for knowledge's sake.

Arguing in such terms cut ice with my scientific colleagues on SRC because the argument is fundamental to the whole practice of natural science, whether it be physical, biological or psychological enquiry. The prime motivation of science lies in the desire to understand the physical world. Contrary to the priorities stated by Karl Marx, scientists give first place to science's power to understand the world, even over technology's power to change it.

Arguing in such terms would have cut ice with theologians also, had they been sitting round the table at SRC. They too are concerned with the search for understanding—though of a more profound Mystery than that of quarks and gluons. Theology has a natural role in an age of science just because it shares with modern science this quest for intelligibility. A theological faculty is a necessary presence in a true university because the search for knowledge is incomplete if it does not include in its aim gaining knowledge of the Creator as well as gaining knowledge of creatures. The unity of knowledge is fractured if theology is excluded. Before I attempt to justify these large claims, it will be helpful to look more closely at the scientific sector of this universal quest for truthful understanding.

The first thing we can learn is the distinction between understanding, on the one hand, and the lesser attainment of explanation, on the other. Quantum theory makes the point most clearly for us. In its modern form it was discovered in the mid 1920s. Since then its techniques have been used daily in many branches of physical science with impressive success. It explains the nature of chemical reactions, the properties of materials, the way the Sun shines. We know how to do the sums and they always seem to come out right. Invented to deal with atoms, quantum theory now makes successful predictions about the behaviour of quarks, which are at least a hundred million times smaller than atoms. At the level of explanation and prediction, it is, perhaps, the most successful scientific theory ever. Yet we do not *understand* it. By that I mean that we are not in a position to feel intellectually content about it, to reckon that we see how it constitutes a totally satisfactory matrix of understanding, whose intrinsic nature and inner consistency we are able to grasp. The problem does not lie in the strangeness of quantum phenomena viewed from our everyday perspective, with their probabilistic character and the unpicturable behaviour in which an entity sometimes appears to show wavelike properties and sometimes appears to show particlelike properties. All that may seem very odd to the commonsense mind, but we have come to see how quantum thinking has to deviate from everyday thinking if it is to accommodate these unexpected possibilities. Once we have grasped that, these counterintuitive properties yield themselves up to being understood in terms of a modified quantum form of intuition. One way of dealing with these seeming perplexities is to recognise that in the quantum world those little logical words 'and' and 'or' have different properties to those that they possess in everyday discourse. It turns out that quantum mechanically, you can mix together possibilities, like 'being here' and 'being there', that we normally think of as being mutually exclusive of each other. The quantum mechanically learned follow their master, Paul Dirac, in calling this the 'superposition principle'.[1]

All that may sound pretty weird, but if you trust what I have said, you can draw from it a useful moral about how to pursue the quest for understanding: 'Do not make common sense the measure of everything but be prepared to recognise aspects of reality in those modes that are intrinsic to their natures, however strange these modes may at first sight seem to be'. There is not one single, simple way in which we can know everything; there is no universal epistemology. We know the everyday world in one way, in its Newtonian clarity; we know the quantum world in another way, in its Heisenbergian uncertainty. Our knowledge of entities must be allowed to conform to the way in which they actually can be known. If we are to meet reality at all, we must meet it on its own terms. If that is a lesson applying to our knowledge of the quantum world, it would not be altogether surprising if it were a principle that also applied to theology's quest for knowledge of the mystery of God.

Once we have grasped the principle of quantum superposition, it turns out, we are also in a position to understand

---

1. See, for example, J. C. Polkinghorne, *The Quantum World* (Penguin, 1990).

the strange duality of wave and particle. Dirac solved this problem through the discovery of quantum field theory. A field is a spread out entity, and so has wave properties, but stirring in quantum theory also produces countable packets of energy (quanta, in fact!), so that there are particle properties as well. The wavelike states are superpositions of states with different numbers of particles, an option impossible in a Newtonian world (where you simply count however many particles you have, and that's that), but perfectly natural in the quantum world.

However, there are other aspects of quantum mechanics that continue to resist our understanding more than seventy years after the theory's original discovery. The most perplexing of these is called 'the measurement problem'. The theory predicts probabilities for various possible outcomes only when a measurement is made on a quantum system. Yet each time such a measurement is actually made, one of these possibilities emerges as the unequivocal result of the experimental observation. How does this definite answer come about? One might attempt to rephrase the question, as Niels Bohr essentially did, by asking, How does the cloudy and fitful quantum world interlock with the clear and determinated world of laboratory equipment? Yet, putting the issue in that form is really begging the question, for there are not two worlds—quantum and laboratory—but one single physical world of which both are aspects. It is humiliating for a quantum physicist to have to admit that currently there is no satisfactory and agreed solution to the measurement problem—a particularly troublesome confession given the fundamental role of measurement in the whole of physics. There is clearly more still to be understood. Another difficulty makes a similar point.

The two great fundamental discoveries of physical science in this century have been quantum theory and the general theory of relativity, which is Einstein's profoundly beautiful and successful account of gravitation. Yet these two theories are imperfectly reconciled with each other. Every attempt so far to combine them has come to grief through the generation of infinite inconsistencies. Most of the time, the problem can be ignored. General relativity is mostly applied to large systems, including the universe itself. Quantum theory is concerned with small-scale behaviour. The normal fields of application of the two theories are thus well separated from each other. However, not only must two such fundamental physical theories eventually find a satisfactory merger for reasons of principle but also those cosmologists, like Stephen Hawking, who are bold enough to talk about the extremely early universe must make some sort of shift at combining them. This is because the cosmos is then so small that it must be treated in a quantum mechanical way. The dazzling speculations with which the quantum cosmologists regale us in their popular books are intellectual arabesques performed on extremely thin theoretical ice. Here is another area of physical science in which understanding is still lacking and where it is much needed.

There is something further we can learn from science's quest for understanding. It is the multi-levelled complexity of reality. The Holy Grail of contemporary particle physics is the so-called Grand Unified Theory (GUT) in which all the fundamental forces of nature might be unified in a description based on a single set of equations — equations so compact that they could be written on your T-shirt, and so beautiful that they would make an intellectually thrilling adornment. So far, the quest, though actively pursued by many very able people, has not succeeded. I certainly wish it well and entertain hopes of its eventual success. However, I begin to dissent when some of my erstwhile colleagues go on in a grandiose way to rename the putative Grand Unified Theory, a 'Theory of Everything'. For that to be true it would be necessary that we had attained a remarkable degree of universal understanding, and that criterion would not even be satisfied within physics itself. A GUT would be an immensely satisfying intellectual discovery but many, many physical phenomena of the highest interest—such as the turbulent motion of fluids, the superconducting properties of metals and the thermodynamic properties of bulk matter—would lie far outside its explanatory range. Conceptually, as well as methodologically, physics cannot be reduced to particle physics. The imperialist claims of a Theory of Everything that asserts it has all within its grasp are no more realistic within physics than are the imperialistic claims of physics outside itself to have all of biology or psychology within its grasp. In turn, it is even less true that science encompasses all that is attainable or significant in the universal quest for understanding.

Galileo encouraged concentration on the primary quantities of matter and motion and a discounting of those secondary qualities, such as colour, that are directly accessible through human perception. Explanations of change were expressed in terms of the mechanical consequences of efficient causes and not in terms of the teleological action of final causes. There is no contesting the brilliant success of this narrow methodological strategy. Limiting the field of view brought into sharp focus certain kinds of phenomena which then yielded up their secrets to the investigating scientist.

Newton's laws of motion and the universal inverse square law of gravity provided a profound, though ultimately (as it turned out) only approximate, understanding of the nature of the solar system. Yet to believe that what had been omitted in order to make these gains had thereby been shown to be insignificant or peripheral would, from the point of view of an adequate understanding of reality, be an altogether unwarranted conclusion. It would amount to mistaking Mr Gradgrind's definition of a horse — 'quadruped, graminivorous, forty teeth, namely twenty-four grinders, four eye teeth and twelve incisive' and so on — for a living animal. A. N. Whitehead would have called it 'the fallacy of misplaced concreteness'.

Let us come straight to the point. A central question is the significance to be assigned to personhood in forming a credible and adequate account of reality. By a person I mean at least this: a self-conscious being, able to use the future tense in anticipation, hope and dread; able to perceive meaning and to assign value; able to respond to beauty and to the call of moral duty; able to love other persons, even to the point of self-sacrifice. To this I would also wish to add an explicit religious dimension arising from the sense of a Reality beyond oneself, without whose gracious sustaining power life is incomplete, a Reality which is the ground of value and being and to whom the proper response is worship and obedience. I believe that we all know ourselves to be persons, even if we do not all wish to label as 'religious' certain aspects of our experience of personhood. Then the question is, What do we make of this phenomenon of personhood? Is the appearance of persons here on planet Earth (and, for all we know, maybe on many other planets elsewhere in the universe) an event of prime significance for the understanding of what is going on, or is it just a curious byproduct of the physiology of certain kinds of animals, so that it is more complicated than, but no more meaningful than, the fact that some animals can digest grass and some cannot? Are we to believe that some animals are self-conscious and some are not, and that's that? To take so dismissive and epiphenomenal a view of personhood seems to be tantamount to denying that there are any meaningful events in cosmic history at all. I cannot conceive of an occurrence in the universe's evolutionary development that is more astonishing and fraught with signs of fruitful significance than that it should have become aware of itself through the coming to be of humanity. Pascal spoke of us as 'thinking reeds', so insignificant on a cosmic scale but yet exceeding all the stars, since we know them and ourselves, and they know nothing. The mystery of consciousness must surely be a deep clue to the mystery of reality. A small but important aspect of this coming-to-be of cosmic awareness is that it permitted the development of science. It is strange, therefore, that some scientists seem to repudiate the insights of consciousness, preferring instead to remain set in the misplaced concreteness of a world of atoms and the void.

If the event of the evolution of persons is a profound pointer to the nature of reality, then science's deliberately chosen self-restriction to impersonally describable phenomena may be methodologically effective but it is metaphysically jejune. The search for understanding will have to be widened to a very considerable degree beyond the limits of purely scientific discourse. In doing so we shall have to learn to discard some intellectual restrictive practices that have been encouraged by that Enlightenment style of thinking of which we are all, to some extent, the heirs. The impersonal is not to be given precedence over the personal, or the quantitative over the qualitative, for they are simply differing aspects of our encounter with a reality whose character is complex and multidimensional and whose different levels can be known only in ways that conform to their distinctive natures. Our study of the experience of doing science has prepared us for such a possibility, with its recognition of the limited role of a reductionist particle physics within the totality of scientific understanding. Reality is too rich to be taken in at a single glance; it must be viewed from many perspectives.

If it is true that the evolution of persons is of prime significance, then it is also true that the personally perceived qualities of reality must be expected to carry a corresponding prime significance. All personal perceptions are, to use a phrase of Thomas Nagel's, 'views from somewhere'.[2] A person has a perspective on the world, with the opportunities for insight and the dangers of deception that every perspective confers. Of course, the same is true of the scientists' perceptions of what they choose to look at, for scientists are persons and I shall argue in the next chapter that this fact is fundamental to the whole scientific enterprise and to its success. Yet the differing perspectives involved in the practice of science are usually rather easily superposed and reconciled—intersubjectively agreed, as we say—with the consequence that the resulting construct has the air of a 'view from nowhere'; it has the air of an 'objective account'.

Once we move on to consider more deeply personal encounters with reality—the perception of beauty, for example—the situation no longer seems so straightforward. There are

2. T. Nagel, *The View from Nowhere* (Oxford University Press, 1986).

differing degrees of individual sensitivity and there are cultural contexts that shape and constrain the reactions of the perceivers. The inexhaustible richness of great art evokes different responses in different people, so that its perception is always a view from somewhere, a personal response. Yet, it seems that there is a sufficient degree of commonality within this range of idiosyncrasy to persuade us that the perception of beauty is an encounter with the way things are, that aesthetic experience offers us a window into reality. This window has its frame—we can only see certain wavelengths of light, hear certain sound frequencies—but it appears that, nevertheless, the opening is wide enough for access to something of great significance. In the search for understanding we must take account of the mysterious fact that the matter of the world, which in the impersonal terms of science has a behaviour that can be described with the crystal clarity of mathematics, is also the carrier of beauty, conveying a personal experience of symbolic power that evades all attempts to reduce it to a restricted and specifiable content, for it always overflows with surplus meaning. If you want to make a materialist reductionist uneasy, ask one what he or she makes of music, and insist on a response that corresponds to the actual way one lives and not to an ideologically glossed version of it. 'Neurological response to vibrations in the air', seems totally inadequate as an account of listening to a performance of the Mass in B Minor.

There are other windows into the multi-levelled character of the world, in addition to science and aesthetics, that afford us insights that must be taken into account in an adequate mapping of the domain of reality. One of the most important is provided by our intuitions of morality. Nowhere is the poverty of a scientistic approach more evident than in the realm of ethical decision.

It has been my privilege to serve on a number of government-appointed committees charged with making recommendations about ethical codes of practice. Often I have been in the chair. The problems we were given to consider derived from advances in medicine and in genetics, areas in which I do not have expert knowledge. Of course, some of my colleagues on these committees were leaders in these fields and we always sought and received opinions and advice from relevant professional bodies and from individual experts. A great weight of scientific evidence was thus accumulated and the fact that I know from the inside how scientists tend to think was helpful to me in evaluating it, even if the technical details were, inevitably, often beyond me. We needed all the understanding we could acquire of the scientific concepts and techniques involved, and of the practical possibilities and their likely consequences, in order to help us in our deliberations. Knowledge is a much better basis for recommendations than ignorance. Yet purely scientific information could not settle the ethical issues. A different kind of insight and understanding was then required. In the search for wisdom in this area, I and my other non-technical colleagues on the committee could contribute on at least equal terms with the scientifically expert members. I say 'at least', because the fact that we were not caught up in the immediate excitement of technical discovery may have given us a degree of helpful detachment, enabling us to recognise that not everything that can be done necessarily should be done, however scientifically remarkable it might be. In these ethical discussions we were no longer a committee of two kinds, experts and non-experts, but a committee of a single kind, a committee of persons, of moral beings in search of wise conclusions.

The universe, composed as it is of quarks and gluons and electrons, is also the carrier of beauty and the arena of moral decision. With the dawning of self-consciousness, not only did there come into being 'thinking reeds' but there also came to be what we might call 'joyful reeds', which perceived and responded to beauty, and 'moral reeds', which acknowledged and obeyed ethical imperatives. Not only do I defend the significance of these different layers of our personal experience, but I also defend their autonomy. I deny that one is basic and the rest are derivable from it. It is the moral imperative that has been subject to the most determined reductionist onslaught in this respect.

Anthropologists draw our attention to the many cultural variations of ethical rules. Of course, we should acknowledge this and take account of it. However, I cannot believe that a morally repellant act, such as the ethnic cleansing of despised minorities through acts of genocide, is properly viewed as being just one conventional choice for the way in which a society might decide to handle its problems. Such evil deeds are not cultural customs but they are absolutely wrong. Sociobiologists of a fairly extreme kind may assure us that what seem to be our moral intuitions are, in fact, genetically imprinted survival strategies. But evolutionary biologists are persons, too, and such a morally reductionist stance is almost impossible to maintain outside the study or the laboratory. In a way, Richard Dawkins is frank about this. He concludes *The Selfish Gene* by saying, 'We are built as gene machines and cultured as meme machines, but we have the power to turn against our creators. We, alone on earth, can rebel against the tyranny of the selfish replicators'.[3] It seems a pity that Dawkins did not go on to ask not only where does this power come from but also what is the source of our urge to exercise it? If he had done so, he might well have concluded that 'person' was a better description for a human being than either 'gene machine' or 'meme machine'.

I believe that there is a further level of experience involved in personhood, widely attested to and of great significance. It is connected with a recognition of human finitude and also with the intuition of an infinite Reality beyond the community of humankind. Death is perhaps one of the most direct ways in which to broach the issue. In one sense, there could be no more obvious illustration of limitation and transience than the thought that death comes to all. 'Golden lads and lasses must, as chimney sweepers, come to dust'. Mortality is universal, for death affects not only human beings and animals but also, on immensely longer timescales, there will be the demise of the Sun and eventually that of the universe itself. Against these sombre facts, however, there is another fact to be set: that deep in the human heart there is an intuition of hope, a belief that the word of death, though certainly spoken, is not the last word. The burial customs of our Neanderthal ancestors suggest that they expected some kind of destiny beyond death. That hope has continued widespread among humankind, though articulated in a great variety of different ways. Some will see this as just a comforting illusion, a strategy diverting attention from the stern fact of individual annihilation, but I do not accept this quick dismissal. For one thing,

3. R. Dawkins, *The Selfish Gene* (Oxford University Press, 1976), 215.

notions of postmortem judgement do not altogether look like dreams of wish fulfilment. If indeed there is a ground for such hope, it can lie only outside the domain of reality directly apprehended by us in this world of transience. If there is a destiny for the finite beyond their finitude, it must surely lie in an infinite and continuing reality. To appropriate a phrase of Thomas Aquinas, that would be a reality 'that all call God'.

Many things could be said about this essentially religious level of experience. Of course, I would want to say them from a Christian perspective, informed by the insights of scripture and of the Church. The hope of a destiny beyond death would then be addressed in terms of the revealed faithfulness of the God of steadfast love and in the light of the resurrection of Jesus Christ. I discussed such issues in my Gifford Lectures[4] and it is not my purpose to repeat that material here. On this occasion I am not attempting either to adjudicate or to persuade in relation to specific theological understandings. Instead, I simply argue that an adequate account of personal experience, either in respect of individuals or in respect of the history of the world, cannot neglect the level of encounter with reality that broadly can be labelled 'religious'. A somewhat regional way of recognising this would be to note how much of the history of Western civilisation is unintelligible without an understanding of the Judaeo-Christian tradition, which permeates its art and culture and informs and shapes its ideas. A number of historians[5] have claimed that even the

---

4. J. C. Polkinghorne, published as *Science and Christian Belief* and *The Faith of a Physicist* (London: SPCK; Princeton: Princeton University Press, 1994).

5. For example, S. Jaki, *The Road of Science and the Ways to God* (Scottish Academic Press, 1978); C. A. Russell, *Cross-Currents* (IVP, 1986).

rise of modern science in seventeenth-century Europe needs as part of its understanding a recognition of the influence of a theological doctrine of creation that affirmed the worth of that creation and emphasised the freely chosen character of the rationality with which the Creator had endowed it. This implied that there was indeed an order to be found in the physical world, but one that could be discovered only by looking and seeing what God had actually chosen to do. The Greek reliance on the power of reason was insufficient; it needed to be supplemented by the insights yielded by experimental observation.

One of the roles of theology in any age is the intellectual study of the religious dimension of personal experience. As with all academic disciplines, that study must be open and honest, prepared to conform to the discovered nature of reality and not shackled by prior prescription of what are the acceptable outcomes of the enquiry. Thus atheism is a possible theological option, provided it arises from consideration of the evidence and not from a preemptive narrowness of prior view. There is a vast—and one must confess, perplexingly varied— body of human testimony down the ages that provides the raw material for this theological quest for understanding. If the religious aspect of personhood has the the significance that I believe is rightly attributed to it, then theological study is an indispensable component of the search for understanding, in a scientific age as much as in any other. I say again, a theological faculty is a necessary part of a university.

To speak of theology in this way is to speak of it as a first-order discipline of enquiry, taking its place alongside science's investigation of the physical world or moral philosophy's investigations of the nature of ethical decision. However, there is a further important role for theology to play, as a second-order reflection upon the whole of human knowledge. To seek to speak of God is to seek to speak of the One who is the ground of all that is. Such discourse, which we might call theological metaphysics, must take account of the first-order insights of science, aesthetics, morality and also, of course, of theology itself in its first-order mode of particular investigation into the understanding and significance of religious experience. Theological metaphysics must respect the integrity of these primary disciplines. It is not its role to instruct them or to correct their conclusions, but to listen to what they have to say about their individual fields of study. The aim of theological metaphysics is the integration of these partial perspectives, afforded by the first-order disciplines, into a single consistent and coherent account of reality. Thereby it seeks to provide a more profound and comprehensive understanding than could be acquired through any single primary mode on its own.

Any scheme of this all-embracing kind has to be based on its chosen and defining explanatory principle, the justification for which must lie in the intelligibility of the resulting account of reality. 'Nothing comes of nothing', and no metaphysics can function without its assumed, and thus unexplained, ground of explanation. *Theological* metaphysics is based on the belief that the will of a self-subsistent divine Agent is the true explanatory principle. If personhood and its qualities have the significance that has been suggested in the course of this chapter, a transpersonal God is surely the more fitting basis for the search for universal understanding than the impersonal power of matter that David Hume and other proponents of physical reductionism recommend to us.

Theological metaphysics naturally accommodates the multi-layered character of reality that we have been considering. Science has many things to tell us. It investigates a physical world whose wonderful order is transparent to our investigation and whose fruitful processes are increasingly understood in terms of an intertwining of order and openness. That world is no piece of cosmic clockwork, for the twentieth century has seen the death of a merely mechanical view of the universe. Both quantum theory and chaos theory portray a more subtle, and I believe more supple, structure than that. In fundamental physics it is an actual technique to seek theories whose expression is in terms of equations endowed with the unmistakable character of mathematical beauty. This is no mere exercise of aesthetic preference, because the experience of three centuries of doing theoretical physics indicates that it is precisely such economic and elegant theories that also exhibit a long-term fruitfulness that is convincing support for the belief that they are verisimilitudinous approximations to physical reality. The more we understand the history of the evolution of life, including the ten-billion-year prehistory in which the necessary chemical elements were being formed in the interior nuclear furnaces of first generation stars, the more we see that the potentiality for this happening had to be present from the start, built into the laws of nature which must take a very precise, 'finely tuned' form if they are to sustain the delicate chain of process that links an expanding ball of energy (the universe post big bang) to the inhabited Earth of today. (I am referring, of course, to the remarkable and unexpected collection of scientific insights that go under the name of the Anthropic Principle.[6]) These are the kinds of things that have become known through scientific discovery.

One might sum it up by saying that we live in a universe whose rational beauty makes it seem a world shot through with signs of mind and that from the beginning was pregnant with the possibility of carbon-based life. That is what science says but, of itself, it can say no more. Yet, if we are people endowed with a thirst for the kind of intellectual satisfaction that comes from gaining understanding through and through, it does not seem sufficient just to treat these remarkable properties as happy accidents. They surely signal the need for a deeper form of intelligibility, going beyond the scientific.

Theological metaphysics can offer us that more profound understanding. The wonderful order of the world is perceived by it as being a reflection of the Mind of the Creator, and the universe's finely tuned aptness to the evolution of life is perceived as an expression of the Creator's fruitful intent. In its turn, theological metaphysics can receive from science important help with one of its most difficult perplexities: the existence of suffering, so widespread in a creation claimed by first-order theology to be good. Science is increasingly aware of the interconnectedness of the processes of the physical world. If some cells are to mutate and produce new forms of life, then other cells will possibly mutate also, but with malignancy the inevitable consequence in their case. The presence of cancer in creation is not due to the Creator's callousness or incompetence; it is the necessary cost of the evolving complexity

6. J. D. Barrow and F. J. Tipler, *The Anthropic Cosmological Principle* (Oxford University Press, 1986); J. Leslie *Universes* (Routledge, 1989).

of life. The whole evolutionary process itself can be understood theologically as the Creator's gift to creation of a due independence, so that it is allowed to explore and realise in its own way the fertility with which it has been endowed. This idea—that an evolutionary universe is a creation 'allowed to make itself'—was part of the immediate Christian reaction to the publication of *The Origin of Species*, being expressed by such clergymen as Charles Kingsley and Frederick Temple. The notion that the Church was unanimous in an obscurantist rejection of Darwin in 1859 is as ignorant and incorrect as is also the belief that the scientific community was unanimous in welcoming him. The black-and-white accounts of those intellectually tempestuous times, so assiduously propagated in the media and in certain kinds of popular scientific writing, are just not true.

I have argued that human appreciations of beauty constitute another level in our encounter with reality, as do our moral convictions and our religious experiences, including those intuitions of hope that arise despite the apparent fact of finitude and transience. In my opinion, no metaphysical scheme that dismisses these aspects of personhood as incidental epiphenomena would be doing justice to the richness of reality. Equally, no metaphysical scheme would be adequate that did not seek to provide an integrated understanding of this multi-levelled encounter with the way things are. How does it come about that the same sequence of events can be a set of physical happenings, yet also the carriers of beauty, moments of moral challenge and decision, opportunities for awareness of the presence of God? For many worshippers, a church service will have all these characteristics and it could not properly be described without taking them all into account. A theistic point of view makes this plenitude of experience intelligible. Just as science's insights of order and potentiality can be understood in the light of the divine Mind and Purpose, so our experiences of beauty can be understood as a sharing in the Creator's joy in creation, our moral intuitions as intimations of God's good and perfect will, our worshipful experiences as discernments of the divine presence, and our hopeful aspirations as grounded in God's unchanging fidelity.

My argument has been based on two assumptions, both of which are congenial to a scientist, so that they ought to find ready acceptance in a scientific age. One is that in forming our account of reality we should be open to all aspects of our encounter with it. Tidy schemes, produced by selective oversimplification and resulting in a neglect of part of the data, are not of any value. Within science itself, this principle meant that in the early years of the twentieth century the physicists had to acknowledge that they had detected both wavelike and particlelike properties in the behaviour of light, however difficult it was to comprehend how these apparently conflicting characteristics could be reconciled with each other. It was an intellectually uncomfortable situation to be in, but ultimately the policy of experiential honesty led to the most profound and exciting discovery about the properties of matter made since the days of Newton. In the wider domain of metaphysical enquiry, the same principle requires us to take seriously all aspects of our experience and to refrain from reaching easy but worthless conclusions by exalting the objective over the subjective, the repeatable over the unique, the impersonal over the personal.

The second presumption is that we live in a cosmos, not a chaos, so that the world makes total sense. In other words, there is indeed a Theory of Everything, but a theory that is much grander and more comprehensive and intellectually satisfying than any Grand Unified Theory of particle physics could ever be. I have been suggesting that the name of that Theory is Theology, that the world makes total sense because it is a creation, the unified expression of the Mind and Will of its Creator. In short, I believe that the search for understanding through and through, if pursued with total openness and honesty, will in the end be found to be the search for God.

That total intelligibility, as far as we are able to glimpse it, must yield not just a contemporary intelligibility, but it must embrace the whole sweep of cosmic history, both past and yet to come. The universe, as cosmologists know it today and extrapolate it into the future, will end in cosmic death, either through collapse or through decay. That recognition seemed to the distinguished theoretical physicist Steven Weinberg to confirm him in his atheism. At the end of his book *The First Three Minutes*, he wrote, 'The more the universe seems comprehensible, the more it also seems pointless'.[7] Weinberg is moved by science's discernment of the rational beauty of the universe but he sees 'futility' written all over its mortal fabric.

There are two ways in which to seek to resolve this tension between science's account of a present universe of wonderful order and cosmology's well-founded prognostications of an ending in eventual chaos. One is the stance of heroic atheism in which humanity defies the meaninglessness with which it is surrounded. Weinberg goes on to express this attitude when he says, 'The effort to understand the universe is one of the very few things that lifts human life a little above the

7. S. Weinberg, *The First Three Minutes* (A Deutsch, 1977), 149.

level of farce and gives it some of the grace of tragedy'.[8] There is a stoic nobility in this stance which I respect, but I believe that it is mistaken. Instead, I choose the theistic resolution of the dilemma posed by cosmic futility, believing that, though the universe will die on a timescale of tens of billions of years, just as you and I will die on a timescale of tens of years, yet we and it have a true hope of a destiny beyond our deaths, assured to us by the faithfulness of the Creator. Theistic metaphysics offers an understanding that embraces the fact of mortality but sets it within the context of a divinely grounded expectation of fulfilment nevertheless. In Christian terms, this hope stems from the resurrection of Christ seen, as Paul understood it, as being the seed of a new creation which is the redemption of the old creation's mortality.

I started this chapter with two assertions fundamental to the life of a university—namely, the value of knowledge for knowledge's sake and a belief in the ultimate unity of all knowledge. Just as the university system of Western Europe historically originated in the setting of the Church's encouragement of learning, so these two foundations of our contemporary life of learning are undergirded by the insights of theological metaphysics. Knowledge is of value because it is the exploration of a created reality, itself given value by the love of its Creator. Knowledge is one because God is one, so that our encounter is with a created unity. The search for understanding is fundamental to our being human, an expression, whether acknowledged as such or not, of a profound obligation to seek for and to honour the Creator.

8. Ibid.

CHAPTER TWO

Motivations for Belief

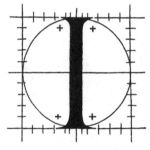

BELIEVE that theology is of continuing significance in a scientific age and that its pursuit is an indispensable part of the activity of a complete university. These claims are based on the perception that theology fulfils two important roles in the spectrum of human enquiry into the way things are. One of these roles is its first-order investigation of religious phenomena, that is to say the encounter with the sacred that is widely attested throughout human history, though in a bewildering variety of ways. In this first role, theology seeks to evaluate the validity of the claims being made in this domain of human experience and to understand the significance that they might carry. The second role of theology is as an integrating discipline, setting the first-order accounts of science, aesthetics, morality, and of religion itself, within a deeper and more comprehensive matrix of understanding. Theological metaphysics, as we may call this activity, aims to be a true 'Theory of Everything', based on the fundamental premise that the Mind and Will of a divine Agent lie behind the multi-levelled character of our encounter with reality.

In the first chapter, my argument concentrated on advocating the adoption of a generous, comprehensive, and non-reductionist account of human experience. In particular, I made a plea to take our personhood seriously, not succumbing to the Enlightenment temptation to esteem the objective above the subjective. For example, we should not exalt science at the expense of art by thinking that the real nature of Giotto's frescos is encapsulated by describing them as collections of fragments of paint of determinate chemical composition, set in a mixture of calcium and silicon oxides.

A critic might object, however, that I had missed the point and that the essential difference between science and theology is not in their differing subject material but in their contrasting methods. The view propounded by this critic might be that science is coolly rational, basing its reliable conclusions on carefully sifted evidence and always willing to revise its opinions if further evidence becomes available that would make this necessary, while theology is doggedly assertive, appealing not to evidence but to unquestionable authority, and so proving immovable in the stance that it takes, whatever the facts may have to say against it. In other words, in this critic's view what we have to deal with would be the open mind of reason contrasted with the closed mind of revelation. Of course, if that were true, then theology's claim to a place in the university curriculum, or its prospects of enduring in a scientific age, would indeed be seriously open to question.

I am afraid that many of my scientific friends who have some sympathy with the idea of a spiritual dimension to life but who feel unable, all the same, to embrace religion, often suppose that something like this is indeed the case with theology. They are not out-and-out reductionists, for they are willing to give some attention to the sort of claims made in the first chapter. They are humane persons, valuing art and respecting morality, and they have a wistful hope that there might be a deeper sense to the universe and its history than science alone has been able to discern. Yet they fear that, were they to pursue this quest for deeper insight by making use of the resources of religion, they would soon find themselves committing intellectual suicide. They expect that they would be faced with a demand to sign on the dotted line to a series of incredible propositions, asserted solely on the basis of some ineffable and unchallengeable source of authority. If that were indeed the case, one could see why they were rightly wary.

I say as clearly and as emphatically as possible that this is not the way theology operates and that the central religious question is the question of truth. Theologians, as much as scientists, are concerned with trying to discern and to understand the nature of reality. They seek to conform their thinking to the way things are. I believe that the best way to try to fulfil that ambition is through the quest for motivated belief and not through submission to unquestionable authority. When I gave up professional work in theoretical physics and eventually became a serious amateur student of theology, I do not think that, in respect to this openness as to what is actually the case, my intellectual attitude changed at all. In the subtitle of my Gifford Lectures I described myself as a 'bottom-up thinker'. By that I meant that my habits of thought, formed by my scientific career, are to try to proceed from evidence to theory, from experience to understanding, and to be very wary of claims to know general principles in advance of particular encounters with reality. No quantum physicist could fail to be other than cautious about our powers of rational prevision.

It is important to recognise, however, that the search for motivated belief is subtle and by no means a straightforward process. The point is best made, in the first instance, by considering the process of scientific discovery itself. In the twentieth century, philosophers subjected the methods of science to intensive scrutiny. It would not be possible to claim that many conclusions have been reached that are widely agreed in the philosophical community or widely recognised as convincing by the scientific community. However, there has been one important gain in understanding. It arises from a widespread acknowledgement that insight is best sought by looking at how it is that science is actually done. Attention is to be focussed first on the activities of scientists, rather than on speculations concerning general epistemological principles. The history of science, including most importantly the contemporary history of science, is an indispensable guide to the philosophy of science. In other words, a spot of bottom-up thinking has become fashionable in this area also. Any notion that science proceeds by the patient accumulation of facts, and their inductive consolidation into established truths, is rapidly dispelled by such an enquiry. A Baconian account of scientific method just does not work.

In brief, there are five insuperable difficulties to so simple a story. The first is that there are no scientifically interesting facts that are not already interpreted facts. Raw registrations recorded in measuring apparatus are of no account on their own, without an understanding of how the instruments work and therefore what it is that they are measuring. Such an understanding can come only from within science itself. Theory and experiment, therefore, inextricably intertwine. There is no impartial view from nowhere, only a perspective from the somewhere of current theoretical insight. Second, all measurements are made in impure regimes, contaminated by effects originating from causes extraneous to those that the experimenter desires to investigate. Scientists call this 'the problem of background' and theory must be used to identify, estimate and allow for these unwanted effects. Third, new theoretical ideas are born in the creative imaginations of their discoverers; they are not just read straight out of nature. Einstein once said that the theoretical basis of physics had to be 'freely invented', originating from flashes of intuitive insight rather than from a plodding Baconian sifting of an assembly of 'for instances'. Fourth, theories always make universal claims going beyond the particularity of what has actually been investigated. The philosophical problems of the justification of induction and of the underdetermination of theory by experiment draw our attention to this mismatch between infinite pretensions and a finite basis of experience. Fifth, there is the historical fact that from time to time, when theories are tested in hitherto unexplored regimes, they are found to need radical revision. In the end, even Newton had to give way to Einstein and Heisenberg.

These five features of scientific endeavour together make it all seem rather a precarious activity. Yet there is another aspect of the actual experience of doing science that also needs to be taken into account. It is the cumulative gain of scientific understanding that gives rise to the belief in the community of scientists that all their wearisome and costly efforts are worthwhile because they are yielding actual knowledge of the nature of the physical world. Theories may in principle be underdetermined by experiment, but when we add to the requirement of wide empirical adequacy the additional criteria for a 'good' scientific theory, that it should be concise and elegant in its formulation, displaying 'naturalness' and avoiding any air of mere contrivance, then, time and again, it both proves initially very difficult to find such a theory and also, when found, that theory proves unique and widely accepted as being the new form of understanding. That this agreement is not just the result of communally imposed intellectual taste, or of a slothful social consensus, seems indicated by the fruitful power of theories of this kind to yield understanding of new phenomena, vastly different from those that gave rise to the theory in the first place. This hallmark of extensive fertile intelligibility is taken by scientists to be the sign that they are in touch with reality. We believe in unseen and unseeable entities, like quarks and gluons, because the assumption of their existence makes sense of great swathes of physical experience. Sustained explanatory power is a convincing encouragement to the belief that science advances by gaining a tightening grip of an actual reality. Of course, that grasp is never complete. The radical changes of understanding induced from time to time through the exploration of new regimes show that science never attains absolute truth but it can, at most, claim only verisimilitude. Scientists are the map-makers of the physical world and, like all careful map-makers, their charts, though not complete in every detail, prove superposable. We understand how the Newtonian map relates on an appropriate scale to the greater detailed accuracy of Einsteinian cartography (see also, chapter 5.1). Every established theory must retain in its own way the successes of its predecessors, as well as going beyond their accounts to new successes of its own.

Science is never absolutely certain, nor is its method absolutely clear cut. Whether they know it or not, whether they like it or not, scientists live in an intellectual world that is rightly called postmodern. The clear and certain ideas of the Cartesian modernist programme have proved to be unattainable, even in its paradigm discipline, natural science. But I believe that science can also help us to live in the postmodern age with integrity and intellectual hope. Contrary to the claims of some of its philosophical and sociological critics, and for the reasons that I have just sketched, science is not driven into a despairing relativism by the collapse of modernity. There *is* a middle way between intellectual certainty and intellectual doubt, between logical guarantees on the one hand and solipsistic individualism or social determinism on the other. This middle way is often called critical realism: 'critical' because it acknowledges the problematics of motivated belief and concedes our inability to rid it of all intellectual precariousness; 'realism' because it recognises, nevertheless, that we can attain a verisimilitudinous grasp of reality.

The most helpful philosopher of this middle way is, I believe, Michael Polanyi. Becoming a philosopher after a long and distinguished career as a physical chemist, he had insights that have been more readily accepted in the scientific community, of which he was an insider, than in the philosophical community, which still seems to treat him as an outsider. His greatest work is *Personal Knowledge: Towards a Post-Critical Philosophy*. He wrote it, he tells us, with the principal purpose of achieving 'a frame of mind in which I may firmly hold to what I believe to be true, even though I know it might conceivably be false'.[1] The key lies in recognising that knowledge is acquired by *persons* and that this feat requires the exercise of tacit skills of judgement (such as are involved in eliminating background effects or—at a higher level—in adjudicating that a proposed theory possesses the characteristics that make it acceptable and scientifically 'good'). These skills are not exhaustively specifiable, for they are not algorithmic. They cannot be reduced to the following of a set of rules, but they have a tacit dimension to them. In consequence, they can be learned only within the convivial practice of a competent community. Polanyi says,

> the *personal participation* of the knower in all acts of understanding . . . does not make our understanding *subjective*. Comprehension is neither an arbitrary act nor a passive experience, but a responsible act claiming universal validity. Such knowing is indeed *objective* in the sense of establishing contact with a hidden reality. . . . It seems reasonable to describe this fusion of the personal and the objective as Personal Knowledge.[2]

I find Polanyi's account of scientific knowing to be recognisable and persuasive. It is the basis of the claim that I made in the first chapter of the importance of the personal in relation to science as well as in relation to other forms of human encounter with reality. To this insight, I add another derived from the Irish-American philosopher of science, Ernan McMullin. He emphasises that critical realism, as exempli-

1. M. Polanyi, *Personal Knowledge* (Routledge and Kegan Paul, 1958), 214.
2. Ibid., vii–viii.

fied by science's power to gain verisimilitudinous knowledge, is to be defended on the historical grounds that this is how it has actually proved to be. Indeed, McMullin speaks of critical realism as something that has been discovered empirically to be the case.[3]

An important point is being made here. A great deal of philosophical discussion is attempting the abstraction, and so the corresponding certainty, associated with the attainment of a universal view from nowhere. It tries to reach conclusions that do not appeal to the specificity of our circumstances. To try to speak of induction under the title of *System of Logic*, as John Stuart Mill did, or to criticise that but then go on to write *The Logic of Scientific Discovery*, as Karl Popper did, is to attempt a discourse that will have validity in all possible worlds. All our actual experience, however, is of the view from the somewhere of the particular kind of world that we inhabit. I think that we need to take this particularity very seriously. It is an actual fact of our experience, whatever may be the case in possible universes in general, that our universe is so constituted, and we are persons so constituted within it, that general verisimilitudinous conclusions can be reached successfully on the basis of finite investigations; that the physical world is remarkably rationally transparent to us; in a word, that science is possible. I do not think that this is likely to be an analytic truth about universes in general, but rather it is a synthetic truth about our universe in particular. Nor, of course, do I think that this is just a happy accident. The deep intelligibility of the world is made understandable for me by the theological

3. E. McMullin in J. Leplin (ed.), *Scientific Realism* (University of California Press, 1984), 8–40.

insight that the universe is a creation and that we, to use an ancient but powerful way of speaking, are creatures made in the image of our Creator.

I believe that this power of persons to achieve verisimilitudinous knowledge of reality extends beyond our scientific encounter with the physical world. Science's experience is that a degree of intellectual boldness in betting on the validity of the understandings we attain is rewarded by our gaining a degree of true insight into the way things are. This should encourage other forms of human enquiry into reality. In particular, it should encourage theology in its first-order task of reflecting on religious experience. If that claim is to be substantiated, we first must reconsider the role that revelation plays in theological thinking. I believe that it bears an analogy with the role played by observations and experiments in science (see also, chapter 3).

The laws of nature operate all the time. However, most physical process is too complex for us to be able to make out what is going on. Understanding is possible only if we have access to regimes that are particularly simple and so particularly transparent to our enquiry. It was good fortune in this respect that enabled modern astronomical theory to get going through the discoveries of Kepler and Newton about the behaviour of the solar system and the nature of gravity. Because planetary orbits are nearly circular and non-intersecting, and because even the largest known planet, Jupiter, has a mass that is only 0.1% of the mass of the Sun, it was possible to gain a great deal of understanding piecemeal, considering one planet at a time in the first approximation. Anything more complicated than that would have produced chaotic motions that generations of Newtons would have been unable to unravel. In terrestrial physics, we are often not so lucky, but it is the art of the experimenter to contrive artificially simple situations in which what is of interest dominates and what is not of current concern can be eliminated or allowed for.

God is always there, just as the laws of nature are always there, but it may well be that there have been particular moments in history that have been unusually open to the divine presence, particular communities unusually responsive to the divine will, particular individuals unusually aware of the divine nature. These transparent occasions and inspired persons are the vehicles of God's self-manifestation, sources of the spiritual insights whose record is what constitutes the revelation preserved in a religious tradition. Such a concept of revelation is one that should not be uncongenial to a scientist. The closer analogy is with the astronomers' observations than with the physicists' experiments, since encounter with the divine cannot be induced or contrived but it can only be received as gracious gift.

Understood in this way, scripture, such as the Bible, is not a kind of divinely dictated textbook laying down the correct answers to the examination questions of life, answers that we had better learn by rote and unfailingly reproduce. Scripture is not an unchallengeable set of propositions demanding unquestioning assent, but it is *evidence*, the record of foundational spiritual experience, the laboratory notebooks of gifted observers of God's ways with men and women. I am not saying, of course, that this evidential approach is the only way in which to read the Bible. Like all profound texts—those classics which have the deep power to speak to us across the centuries, fusing the 'two horizons' [4] of past and present—the Bible can be read in many ways and at many levels. There is a spiritual way of reading in which we submit ourselves to its interrogation, rather than submitting its pages to our critical scrutiny. Many testify to the power of scripture read in this way, and such a reading is central to my own spiritual life. Nevertheless, the Bible is also evidence, without which we would know next to nothing about ancient Israel and next to nothing about Jesus Christ, a people and a person whose influence has been fundamental to the formation of Western civilisation and who still have to be reckoned with in this scientific age.

In a similar way, the Christian creeds are not non-negotiable formulae presented for us to sign without hesitation or question. Instead, they are concise summaries of the Church's beliefs, arising from its intense reflection on the foundational events recorded in scripture and the continuing experiences of worship and obedience present in the lives of its members, who are seeking to live in the faith of the risen Christ. These credal statements are very concise (there are only 227 words in the standard English translation of the Nicene Creed) and I have compared them elsewhere to the data tables that all particle physicists carry in their pockets, summaries of what we have come to know. Yet each generation has to make the creeds its own, bringing to them its own insights and its own perplexities.

This last remark points us to an important difference between science and theology. The data tables of the particle physicists change as new discoveries are made or as measure-

4. A. Thiselton, *The Two Horizons* (Paternoster Press, 1980).

ments become more accurate. But, after a sufficiently long winnowing process, each section of the tables will acquire a lasting stability. Science is cumulative; it conquers intellectual territory that it will not have to give up thereafter. The average physics Ph.D. of today has a vastly better understanding of the physical world and its processes than Sir Isaac Newton ever did. This progressive increase of knowledge arises from science's transcendence of its subject material, expressed most clearly in the interrogative power of experiment to put matters to the test. It results in an ability to reach verisimilitudinous conclusions that will continue to stand in the circumscribed domain in which they have been thoroughly tested.

Theology is not cumulative in this way. Its Subject transcends human observers; the transpersonal reality of God is not open to our manipulation or putting to the test. Each generation has its own experience of God and its own insights into the divine nature, but there is no presumptive superiority of a twentieth-century view over the understandings of past centuries. That is why theologians maintain a constant dialogue with the past—Paul and Augustine and Aquinas and Calvin are their continuing conversation partners—while scientists, however respectful they rightly are of the achievements of Newton and James Clerk Maxwell, live very much in the present. In the sphere of religious knowledge, the English mystics of the fourteenth century, like Julian of Norwich or the anonymous author of *The Cloud of Unknowing*, may well have had spiritual understanding that is attenuated or lost in our very different society today, and which we can recover only by making ourselves apprentices to their insights.

At first, there might seem to be a difficulty here. I am maintaining that theological understanding is not the sole possession of any one generation, and that all that is needful is not necessarily in the hands of the contemporary. Rather, under-standing is spread over many generations, with each adding its own contribution, arising from its own perspective. There is, therefore, a need to seek some sort of integration of these diverse and varying insights. Yet we cannot honestly suppose that we have the power to become transtemporal thinkers. The resolution lies in recognising that, while we need release from the cultural prisonhouse of our own time — a release that can only come from continuing interaction with the ages that have preceded ours — we can only make their insights our own in our own way.

The intellectual scene thus described is fluid, interactive, dynamic rather than static. A paradox might seem to arise when this account is compared with the unchanging character of credal formulae. The Nicene Creed of the churches today is exactly the same as that which was endorsed at the second Oecumenical Council of Constantinople in 381. How can an unchanging text be reconciled with continuing enquiry and the assertion that each generation has to make the Creed its own? The answer lies in recognising the character of credal statements. They are concise precisely because they do not seek to be exhaustively specific. Their purpose is not to define a point-like pinnacle of orthodoxy on which all must perch and from which it would be fatal to deviate by an inch. Rather, they stake out a territory within which a faithful theology is free to roam. This concept of openness within limits is essen-tial to theology. The mystery of God cannot be tied down to a series of precise propositions, but neither is it the case that 'anything goes'. As the late Ian Ramsey liked to remind us, theological language is human language that is 'stretched' in some way in the effort to do some kind of justice to encounter with the infinite reality of God.[5] That stretching has to be in the right direction. When we speak of God as personal, we certainly mean something going beyond the finite limits of human personality. We use such language, not because it is fully adequate, but because it is less misleading to use personal terms about God than it is to use impersonal terms. God is more like 'Father' than like 'Force', though we know we are not talking about an old man in the sky. The need for statement without narrow definition is why the open language of symbol is the natural language of theological discourse, in contrast to the precise language of mathematics, which is the natural language of discourse in physical science.

Perhaps I can illustrate how theology attempts to articulate its motivated beliefs by sketching some considerations relevant to a central Christian concern: How are we to understand the significance of Jesus Christ?[6] We can see the discussion starting in the pages of the New Testament. Three of its most creative writers wrestle with the problem of how it is fitting to speak of him. Paul frequently brackets Jesus and God together, using phrases like 'God the Father and our Lord Jesus Christ'. He calls Jesus 'Lord' more than two hundred times, making use of a title that would have had distinct divine overtones for Jews, who used the Hebrew equivalent *Adonai* as a way of referring to God without using the unutterable divine Name. Yet Paul, as a monotheistic believer in the God of Israel, refrains from saying out and out that Jesus is divine.

5. I. T. Ramsey, *Religious Language* (SCM Press, 1957).

6. Cf. J. C. Polkinghorne, *Science and Christian Belief/The Faith of a Physicist* (SPCK/Princeton University Press, 1994) chs. 5–7; *Belief in God in an Age of Science* (Yale University Press, 1998), ch. 2.

John expresses his understanding in the timeless discourses attributed to Christ in his gospel, in which Jesus is portrayed as affirming his unity with the Father, though he also says 'My Father is greater than I' (John 14:28). The unknown author of the Epistle to the Hebrews clearly states Jesus' solidarity with humanity in suffering and testing but also tells of his exaltation to be our Heavenly High Priest and speaks of him as bearing 'the very stamp of [God's] nature, upholding the universe by his word of power' (Heb. 1:3). In their three different ways, these writers show that they are driven to use divine language about Jesus, as well as human language, if they are to do justice to their experience and understanding of him. What this could mean is largely unresolved in the New Testament. The Christological problem is stated there, but it is not solved. One could say the same, I think, about the famous Definition issued by the fourth Oecumenical Council at Chalcedon in 451. It stated most clearly that adequate Christian understanding must wrestle with the need to recognise both human and divine natures in Christ, without specifying a theory of how this combination of the finite and the Infinite was to be understood. It sought to set boundaries to the area of discourse within which faithful Christological thinking should be contained, but it did not provide a detailed map of the terrain.

I am trying to make two points. One is that Christian theological discourse is not cut and dried, utterly prescriptive and allowing no room for subsequent intellectual manoeuvre. On the contrary, it encourages a diversity of contributions, while at the same time it sets limits to the range of possibilities that the Church can recognise as adequate to its experience. These limitations arise precisely from theology's quest for *motivated* belief rather than indulging in unbounded speculation; they are the theological equivalents of the requirements of empirical adequacy that set limits to the range of acceptable scientific theories. And that is my second point: Christian theology should be understood as a bottom-up response to religious experience, the search for a set of motivated beliefs.

Let us continue to consider Christology a little further. I think that one can discern two principal constraining factors which determine the adequacy of any discussion that could fittingly be called Christian. One is provided by the resurrection of Christ. There is, of course, a variety of ways in which Christians have sought to understand this unique event, whose character is both historical and transhistorical. The forms of these understandings are subject to the need to be loyal to the central affirmation of Christian experience, expressed in the conviction 'Jesus lives!'. The motivations for that conviction would require careful and extensive consideration. I made my contribution to this discussion in my Gifford Lectures[7] and I will not repeat that here. Let me be content just to say this: When we compare Jesus with other great spiritual leaders, the founders of world faiths, then there are a number of similarities but there is also one very important difference. They—Moses, Buddha, Mohammed—all die in honoured old age, surrounded by disciples resolved to carry on the work and message of the Master. Jesus dies in mid-life, painfully and shamefully executed, deserted by his followers and with a cry of dereliction on his lips, 'My God, my God, why have you forsaken me?' It seems the story of total and utter failure. If that really was where the story of Jesus ended, I think we would never have heard of him. His life would have

7. See Polkinghorne, *Belief/Faith*, ch. 6.

been that of a wandering preacher and miracle-worker whose significance proved in the end as transient as that of others of that kind who roamed the lands of the Eastern Mediterranean some two thousand years ago. Such people soon disappear from view. That has not happened to Jesus. He remains someone with whom, even today, we all have to reckon. *Something* happened to prolong his story and bring it to us down through the centuries. I believe it was his resurrection from the dead.

A second constraint on any Christological understanding is that it should do justice to the experience of Jesus' followers from the first century to the present day, that the encounter with Christ brings with it an enabling and transforming power. The Christian testimony is that from Jesus we receive not just moral advice about how to live the good life, or even the example of such a life, but also the power by which to live out that life. The experience of the first disciples that their faith in the risen Christ had brought them this new way of living was one of the reasons why they felt driven to believe that the life of God was present in him in a totally unique way.

Clearly these claims need much more extensive and careful consideration than I can give them here, but I hope I have said enough to indicate that Christian belief is not irrational assertion but it is motivated by Christian experience. What I have called the Christological constraints are the equivalent of a scientist's evaluation of what are the phenomena that a new theory must be able to comprehend. However, scientific belief is not only motivated, it is also fruitful, convincing us by its power to yield understanding of phenomena beyond the range of those that led to the original formulation of the theory. Could theology conceivably make a similar claim? I think that it can, within the limits of the necessarily more partial understanding that finite beings can have of the infinite reality of God. Let me give you three examples.

The first relates to the most difficult of all theological perplexities, the problem of evil and suffering. I suggested in the first chapter that science gives theology some modest help by its recognition that an evolving world cannot be a world free from malfunctions or extinctions. However, the existential challenge of evil is too profound to be met solely by so coolly rational an argument. In the century of the Holocaust, the problem was rightly felt with a peculiar intensity. In response, Christian theology discovered that its doctrine of the incarnation, its belief in God's true presence in the humanity of the crucified Jesus even to the point of the paradoxical experience of the depths of God-forsakenness in the darkness of Calvary, yields an insight into a God who is not just a compassionate spectator of creation's travail, but a fellow-sufferer within it. In the late middle ages, also a time of very widespread human pain and anguish, much Christian devotion centred on Jesus recognised as the Man of Sorrows. In the twentieth century, it was the profound image of the Crucified God that spoke to the deepest levels of Christian struggle with the terrible fact of evil. That image, so movingly presented in the work of Jürgen Moltmann that bears that title,[8] does not explain away the problem of suffering but it encounters it at the depth that its mystery demands. The central Christian concept of the incarnation, of a God who truly shares in creaturely life, proves a rich source of continuing and developing theological insight.

My second example concerns theology's power to relate

8. J. Moltmann, *The Crucified God* (SCM Press, 1974).

to and illuminate a twentieth-century development in scientific understanding of the nature of the physical world. The Newtonian picture was of space as an empty container within which separate and individual particles collided and coalesced with each other in the course of a history characterised by the even flow of universal time. Twentieth-century science has replaced this atomistic account by something altogether more integrated and relational. Einstein's theory of general relativity links together space, time and matter in an inseparable relationship. Physicists have discovered that in the quantum domain there is a counterintuitive 'togetherness-in-separation' (what we formally call, non-locality or entanglement) which means that once two entities have interacted with each other, they subsequently retain a power of mutual influence, however widely they might have become separated. This EPR effect (named acronymically after its original proposers, Albert Einstein, Boris Podolsky and Nathan Rosen) has been verified experimentally as being a property of nature. In a fascinating antireductionist twist, it turns out that the subatomic world cannot be treated atomistically. A similar conclusion has been reached for many phenomena taking place at the level of everyday physical process. Chaos theory shows that most systems are not reliable mechanical 'clocks', but rather they are 'clouds', so sensitive to circumstance that the slightest disturbance will totally change their future behaviour. Entities of this degree of delicacy can never be isolated from the effects of their environment. A calculation shows that to predict whether an air molecule in a room will, after a minute fraction of a second, be moving towards the back wall or away from it, would require the literally universal knowledge of the location of every electron in the observable universe, so sensitive are such motions, even over very short periods of time, to the details of circumstance.

Scientists and philosophers are still struggling to grasp all the implications of the astonishing degree of relationality that has been discovered to be present in the physical world. Theologians, however, can readily take it on board, for they have long known the interconnected and interrelated nature of reality. At the heart of their understanding is the Christian doctrine of the Trinity, not a curious piece of mystical arithmetic equating 3 and 1, but a recognition that the inner nature of God, the One who is the ground of all reality, is relationship between three divine Persons. This insight has been better preserved and pursued within the Eastern Church than within the Latin Church of the West. A leading Orthodox theologian John Zizioulas has written a fine book with the title *Being as Communion*.[9] One could paraphrase that as 'Reality as Relationship'.

My third example has no scientific analogue. Religious insight involves not simply the provision of answers to intellectual questions; it also involves the transformation of the life of the questioner. My firm belief in quarks and gluons leaves most aspects of my life untouched. My committed Christian belief must have moral consequences for all that I am and do. Jesus put it with characteristic simplicity and directness, 'You will know them by their fruits'. Here is a different kind of test of fertility, one that is intrinsic to the whole character of the religious life. No one could pretend that applying it yields im-

9. J. Zizioulas, *Being as Communion* (Darton, Longman and Todd, 1985).

mediate and unambiguous conclusions. We have to consider the application of the test both at the level of individuals and of communities.

All of us can think of people of orthodox belief who are fearful in their encounter with reality and mean-spirited in their treatment of others. But perhaps these are 'background effects', as a scientist would put it, resulting from persons whose lives have been distorted or impoverished by causes of which we are unaware and for which religion does not pretend to produce a magic cure, causes such as an unsympathetic upbringing or concealed ill-health. We can also all think of people of no religious faith whatsoever who display a generosity and compassion that is very attractive. Yet I would have to say, both concerning those whom I have known personally and also those historical characters of whom I have some acquaintance, that an impressive proportion of the most wise and good and trustworthy are people of religious faith. I shall not attempt a catalogue but let me just say that I suppose that one of the most widely admired people of recent times has been Mother Teresa of Calcutta.

At the community level a similar degree of ambiguity has to be acknowledged. The history of the Church contains many episodes—crusades, inquisitions, forcible conversions —for which Christians can feel only a penitent sorrow. Yet there are countermovements to be set against these terrible deviations. The time of the Fourth Crusade in Egypt was also the time when Francis of Assisi denounced the excesses of the crusaders, crossed the military lines and had a long conversation on spiritual matters with the Sultan, who was deeply impressed, though not converted. It seems that the Body of Christ has its own spiritual immuno-suppressive system to counteract the effects of infection by demonic distortion. It would be ungrateful and ungenerous for universities and hospitals not to acknowledge the Christian Church's role over the centuries in fostering learning and providing for the care of the sick.

Religion, therefore, has its claims to fruitfulness. Unlike science, and for reasons we have already discussed, theology's search for understanding does not have the character of a steady accumulation of universally agreed results but, nevertheless, it is not without its revisionary advances. The pace of change may be slow—it took eighteen centuries to recognise that slavery is repugnant to the Christian conscience and a little longer to question whether a loving God imposes on finite beings the punishment of eternal torture—but there have been lasting gains in theological understanding. As for comprehensiveness—another quality much prized by scientists in their search for 'good' theories—I contend in chapter 1 that theology in its second-order role of theological metaphysics has a sustainable claim to the title of a Theory of Everything.

My defence of theological understanding as providing the kind of motivated belief that can alone expect to command respect in a scientific age is coming to its end. I have sketched the kind of case that might be made by the community of Christian theologians. Were that community the whole of the theological world, my task would be concluded. But that, of course, is not the case. In contrast to the unified and worldwide scientific community, there is a largely regional collection of disparate theological communities, mostly Christian or Jewish in Europe and North America, mostly Moslem in the Middle East, mostly Hindu in India, mostly Buddhist in much of East Asia, and so on. In contrast to the unanimity of the scientists on such fundamental issues as the existence of quarks and gluons or the molecular basis of genetics, there is no unanimity in the theological world even about so fundamental an issue as the existence of one true God—Theravada Buddhism appears at best agnostic on the question. If theological beliefs are motivated beliefs, why are such contrasting convictions generated in these different communities? Is human destiny beyond death reincarnation, resurrection or reabsorption in the ocean of being? Is the human self of unique and lasting significance, or is it an illusion from which to seek release?

I can do little more than acknowledge the problem and say that I regard it as one of the most urgent and critical items on the contemporary theological agenda.[10] The complexity and subtlety of the great world faith traditions mean that this is a problem that cannot be expected to yield a quick and easy solution. No doubt, differing cultural histories and perspectives are the source of some of these differences of understanding and symbolic expression, but I do not think that this factor alone is sufficient to explain the apparently dissonant variety of the world faiths. Some theologians believe that they can discern beneath the bewildering cognitive conflicts, a basic substrate of encounter with sacred Reality and a common call to human self-transcendence. There is too much work yet remaining to be sure whether this is indeed the case. Let me content myself by saying two things. The first is that religious understanding must start within a tradition, taking with great seriousness the experience and insight that tradition pre-

10. See Polkinghorne, *Belief/Faith*, ch. 10; *Belief in God*, 111–113.

serves. Once again, there is no accessible view from nowhere, only a perspective from somewhere. That is why I am self-confessedly writing from a Christian point of view. I can do no other. The second point is the complement to the first, namely, that if theology is to be true to its essential nature as a search for truthful understanding, then these issues will not be pursued by means of each tradition stridently reasserting the total correctness and adequacy of its own exclusive point of view, but by a truth-seeking dialogue between the traditions, long and painful and difficult as that will surely be. The quest for motivated belief will take on a further dimension when it is pursued in the setting of this truly ecumenical meetingplace. There is a vital necessity that we should be willing to continue on this shared long search for the deepest truth about reality.

CHAPTER THREE

The Role of Revelation

OR good or ill—and no doubt it is a mixture of both—my habits of thought are strongly influenced by my experience of working for many years as a theoretical physicist. I have already explained in chapter 2 that I believe the search for motivated belief is as of as much concern to the religious person as it is to the scientist. That is why I am able to be both. In the course of the argument, I made the claim—which may seem to some readers an outrageous piece of theological coat-trailing—that 'revelation bears analogy with the role played by observations and experiments in science' (p. 36). I have written about revelation in these terms before.[1]

It is clear to me, however, from conversations and certain reviews of my books, that suspicion still lurks in the minds of

1. J. C. Polkinghorne, *Reason and Reality* (SPCK, 1991), chs. 4 and 5; *Science and Christian Belief/The Faith of a Physicist* (SPCK/Princeton University Press, 1994), ch. 2.

many. They seem to think that religious believers enter into intellectual discussion with the ace of trumps of revelatory certainty hidden up their sleeves and with the brazen claim that it is the Holy Spirit who has put it there. There is no denying, of course, that some believers operate in this way. 'The Bible says . . .', or 'It is written in the Holy Qur'an . . .', immediately settles an issue for them. My respect for the depth and subtlety of scripture, together with the recognition that God-inspired utterances still remain humanly articulated utterances, does not allow me to use it in such a propositionally deterministic way. But why use it at all? some may say. What could be the continuing significance of writings some two to three thousand years old, originating in a small and fairly obscure community close to the Eastern shores of the Mediterranean? Such historical and geographical particularity is surely far too limiting to produce something of universal relevance.

Two kinds of response could be made, the one broad in character, the other more specific. The broad point is to challenge the scientist's innate inclination to favour generality over specificity and at the same time to question the assertion that the repeatable is always a more reliable source of evidence than the unique. Of course, the power of repetition carries with it (in principle and to some degree in practice) the possibility of general access to confirmation. If you do not believe that moving a magnet around in the presence of a copper wire will induce a current in the circuit, then try it for yourself and see that this is so. You do not have to take Michael Faraday's word for it. If you do not believe in W and Z particles, you will probably have to take Carlo Rubbia's word for it, since you will not be able to build an electron-positron collider in your back garden, but at least his results have been confirmed by colleagues with access to similar facilities. However, if you want to gain support for your favoured version of a Grand Unified Theory, it is only the unique regime of the very early universe (itself accessible only through rather precarious conjectures about what was going on then) that will afford access to processes occurring at energies high enough to manifest grand unification effects.

Even in laboratory science there is an important role for very specific regimes, often characterised by extreme values of certain parameters. I spent several years working on models of deep inelastic scattering. These phenomena consist of processes taking place at high energies and with large transfers of momentum between the colliding particles. It turned out that these conditions greatly simplified the kind of behaviour one might expect to find and this made them much easier to analyse than more ordinary scattering events, which are confusingly complex in character. Deep inelastic scattering played an important part in convincing physicists of the reality of the quark structure of matter, despite our inability to exhibit isolated quark constituents directly. The pursuit of simplicity through extremity is a powerful technique in physical science.

It would not be surprising, therefore, if extreme and unusual religious experiences, such as the mystic's experience of unity with the One, or the contrasting numinous encounter with a Reality mysterious and fascinating in its otherness, provide particularly significant revelatory insights into the nature of the sacred, despite their comparative rarity. There is a role for unique regimes within the impersonal domain of science, and so we may expect that also to be the case within the realm of personal and transpersonal experience with which religion is concerned. One of our principal sources of understanding of what it means to be human is given us through the great literature of the world. Often it is apparently secular in its character, though I believe that in reality it is based on hidden foundations in the sacredness of life.[2] Literature's deepest insights do not come from tales of a generalised Everyman figure, but from the specificities of an Emma Woodhouse or an Alyosha Karamazov.

When we turn from the content of science to the practice of science, a similar recognition of the role for the unique becomes apparent. I have already concurred with Michael Polanyi's judgement that science is irreducibly an activity of persons. While the role of honest toilers in the scientific community is certainly important, it is not possible to give a just account of the history of scientific discovery without also acknowledging the prime role of the men and women of genius whose deep insight has propelled their subject into its next great phase of advance.[3] Albert Einstein in the Patent Office in Berne, brooding on the nature of space and time, or Werner Heisenberg on Heligoland recovering from a bout of hay fever while wrestling with the perplexities of atomic spectra, represent unique episodes in the history of physics. Because science is also driven by the nudge of nature, one could not claim that special relativity or quantum theory would have remained undiscovered without these two men. (After all, Erwin Schrödinger, another man of genius, was hot foot on the track of his wave mechanical version of quantum mechanics.) But one can

2. Cf. G. Steiner, *Real Presences* (Faber and Faber, 1989).

3. Cf. J. C. Polkinghorne, *Beyond Science* (Cambridge University Press, 1996), ch. 4.

say that progress would have been slow and piecemeal without the intuitive insights and creative leaps of the imagination of these geniuses.

Great scientists have the gift of seeing the one thing needed at the time to advance their subject and of seeing it with clarity and concentration. One could say the same thing about notable prophetic figures within the history of religion. Jeremiah saw with painful precision that Judah was under God's judgement because of its apostasy, that Egypt would not save it from the invading Babylonian armies and that the best hope lay in making what terms it could with Nebuchadnezzar (Jeremiah 36–44). It was an unpalatable message, rejected by his contemporaries. No doubt, in time lesser men, such as Gedaliah, came also to see, in a slow and piecemeal way, that this was so, but by then the inexorability of history had made it too late.

Broad considerations of this kind suggest that it would be unreasonable to reject the possibility that a record of particular people and particular events might be of unique importance in theology's quest for an understanding of the nature of ultimate reality. To this general argument can be added a further and more specific consideration. It arises from the actual experienced power of scripture to speak across the centuries, and across all the many cultural changes that intervene, to enlighten us in our day in ways that are meaningful and powerful. The fact of continuing study of the Bible by many people is something to be taken into account. In many ways it might seem astonishing that this venerable literature is still read with attention and spiritual profit when so many things have changed since its writing. After all, the great nation of

Jeremiah's day was obviously the revived Babylonian empire and the great contemporary figure was its king, Nebuchadnezzar. It would have greatly surprised the people of that day to learn that, two and a half millennia later, one of the main reasons the Babylonians and their monarch are remembered is because they intervened in the affairs of that second rate state, Judah. And Judah is known today because, imperfectly and often unfaithfully, it had a knowledge and experience of God that still seems relevant to us. This is a remarkable reversal of what would have seemed the realities of the time. Persistence of a people and their writings is a phenomenon that is worth investigating. It calls for explanation. Once, when someone was asked for evidence of the existence of God, he simply replied 'the Jews'. The survival of this race, despite its many setbacks and terrible persecutions, is something to be understood. The idea that God revealed something of the divine nature in and through this people is a hypothesis that should be given serious consideration.

Similar arguments apply to the New Testament period. Jesus was a wandering preacher and healer who wrote no book and who died a painful and shameful death, deserted by his followers. Why is it that we have heard of him and that he is still someone to be reckoned with, by Christian believer and by unbeliever alike?

Answers in terms of sheer historical accident, or the stubborn persistence of entrenched positions, seem inadequate to the phenomena. The possibility of revelation, of God made known through persons and events, is one that deserves a place on any agenda of rational enquiry. It is not my present purpose to argue that this is in fact the right assessment, though that is what I believe and what I have defended elsewhere.[4] I simply wish to suggest that recourse to the Bible as a source of knowledge about God is not a strategy of superstition, fideism or obscurantism but a proper part of reasonable theological enquiry. Appeal to revelation is not the closure of theological discussion but the ground of its initiation.

So far I have been speaking of revelation as evidence on which a theological understanding can be based. Treated in this mode, it consists of material that is to be subjected to our investigation. If it is to motivate our belief, it must first be subjected to tests of its reliability. What is the trustworthiness of the gospels in their accounts of the words and deeds of Jesus? How are we to evaluate the stories that he was seen alive after his death and that the tomb was found empty? There are clearly stories in the Bible (Adam and Eve in the garden) that convey deep truth through imaginative narrative, but which we do not have to believe are matter-of-fact historical occurrences. How are we to tell myth from history, and to what extent does the discrimination matter? These are again questions that I have attempted to address elsewhere,[5] and it is not necessary now to attempt to repeat that discussion in detail. It is an analysis that cannot take a general form but it must concern itself with the assessment of the particular instances under consideration. Nevertheless, there are some general characteristics that feature in any specific treatment of these questions.

There is an inescapable tension involved between, on the one hand, the acknowledgement that uniquely significant

4. Polkinghorne, *Belief/Faith.*
5. Ibid.

events may well have about them unusual or unprecedented characteristics which are part of the reason for believing them to carry a revelatory significance and, on the other hand, the recognition that also there must be some degree of resonance with ordinary human experience if these events are to be intelligible to later generations. There must be an element of novel disclosure present, but of such a form that what had previously been dimly perceived or hoped for is now seen clearly to be the case. Thus the resurrection of Christ, though an event *sui generis*, can also be understood as confirming a deep human intuition that death shall not ultimately have the last word. This revelatory dimension corresponds to the understanding conveyed in St John's gospel that miracles are 'signs' — not divine tours de force in which God shows off divine power, but windows into a deeper view of reality than would otherwise be visible. [6] There are some analogies here with the scientific exploration of a new regime of physical experience. Quite unexpected and puzzling phenomena can show up, but eventually they must be relatable to phenomena that are already familiar. The discovery of superconductivity at low temperatures cast new light on the behaviour of electrons in metals, but ultimately it had to be capable of being correlated with the ordinary phenomena of conduction for which Ohm's law had proved so reliable a guide at ordinary temperatures.

However important specific revelatory experiences may be, theological discourse cannot centre exclusively on unusual events in which the divine presence and activity may most clearly be seen. It must also have as its concern the ambiguities that characterise so much else of life and history. In Isra-

6. See J. C. Polkinghorne, *Science and Providence* (SPCK, 1989), ch. 4.

elite terms, theology must concern itself not only with the Exodus deliverance from Egypt but also with the more perplexing events of the destruction of the Temple and the Exile into Babylon. In ordinary human terms, it must concern itself not only with miracles of healing but also with the many sad cases in which physical recovery is earnestly desired but not forthcoming. In its interrogative mode, theology must consider not only the edifying but also the baffling and disturbing. One of the striking features of ancient Jewish encounter with God is the frankness with which protest and puzzlement are expressed, particularly in the Psalms. 'Why, O Lord, do you stand far off? Why do you hide yourself in times of trouble?' (Psalm 10:1). A robust theology will not recoil from the painful questions of theodicy.[7]

Yet, theology cannot conduct the whole of its discourse in a questioning and challenging mode. That is because all intellectual search for understanding must be conformed to, and seek to respect, the nature of the entity being considered. Christians certainly have reason to believe that God will honour the integrity and honest intent that lead to wrestling with the perplexities of a world both fruitful and painful in its character, but we have reason also to believe that true encounter with God will be characterised by awe and obedience. Receiving revelation will not only involve evaluating evidence but also it will involve an acceptance of what is given and an appropriate response to the gift. Faith in God is not simply an intellectual strategy of metaphysical explanation; it is a commitment of life involving the person at all levels of being. There is, therefore, both an active and a passive component in

7. Ibid., ch. 5.

the human response to revelation. The way that the balance is struck between investigation and reception, challenge and acceptance, mind and heart, will have a decisive effect upon the kind of theological thinking that will result.

Those of us whose intellectual formation has been in science will tend to be questioning activists in our response to revelation. I have already emphasised its evidential role. We are thinkers 'from the bottom up'. Did it happen? What can it mean? are the questions on our agenda. Natural theology is an important pursuit for us. We do not suppose that we can *prove* God's existence from the order and fertility of the universe (any more than we can strictly prove the existence of the unseen quarks), but we would be troubled if we did not feel we could discern some 'hints of divinity' in what we know about the structure and history of the cosmos. The tone of our writings, at best, tends to be cooly rational—persuasive, we hope, because of its appeal to the deeper intelligibility that theism affords in its account of a unified view of knowledge. Among the critics of this kind of response it is often thought that the passion and beauty of the encounter with God has been drained out by its kind of senior common room reasonableness. The existential realities of the religious life's costly commitment and sustaining hope have not been given their due. Scientist-theologians like myself have to take these criticisms seriously.

What one might call the passive accepting response to revelation emphasises the humble and obedient reception of the Word that God has spoken. Its thinking is 'from the top down'. It looks askance at those human efforts, such as natural theology, that attempt to climb the foothills of the divine from the plain of common experience and under the guidance of

reasonable enquiry. In the twentieth century, the whole movement stemming from Karl Barth was a powerful expression
of this understanding of the primacy of revelation as given. It
does not deny the value of the human intellect but it places a
low assessment on its relevance to matters divine. It does not
deny the value of secular modes of human rational enquiry but
it believes that they have little to offer to the distinctive theological task.

It seems clear that either approach, if pursued in isolation,
can lead to serious distortion. Theology cannot rightly proceed either as if God were just yet another object of enquiry, or
as if its proper place was in a fideistic ghetto, walled-off from
other forms of knowledge. A striking example of the intertwining of the two approaches is contained in the book of Job.
In chapters 3 to 37 there are long arguments between Job and
his friends about the significance of the disasters that have be-
fallen him and his family. The friends are sure that they are
God's punishment for secret sins in Job's past and they urge
him to acknowledge that this is so. For his part, Job protests
that this is not true and he longs to put his case to God directly: 'But I would speak with the Almighty and I desire to
argue my case with God' (Job 13:3). There are passages of bit-
ter protest at the heaviness of the blows that have fallen on
him: 'I was at ease, and he broke me in two; he seized me by
the neck and dashed me to pieces' (Job 16:12). The arguments
ebb and flow and their mode is clearly that of active questioning. In chapter 38, the Lord begins to speak to Job from out of
the whirlwind. The longed-for confrontation between distant
deity and suffering humanity is taking place, but its form is
quite different from what might have been anticipated on the
basis of what had gone before. God simply points Job to the

majesty of creation and the plurality of the divine concerns with what is going on therein. Referring to a mythical monster who symbolises non-human life, the Lord says 'Look at Behemoth, which I made just as I made you' (Job 40:15). The detailed perplexities of the preceding discussion are left unaddressed, yet it seems that the passive acceptance of the revelation of the divine presence is a sufficient answer for Job. 'I had heard of you by the hearing of the ear, but now my eye sees you; therefore I despise myself and repent in dust and ashes' (Job 42: 5-6).

The poetic account of these chapters is set within a prose story of yet another character. It begins with a wager in the heavenly court between the Lord and Satan about whether Job will remain faithful and not deny God, even if he loses his family and his flocks and herds. It ends with Job being 'compensated' by raising a second family and the restoration of his flocks and herds, doubled in size. This is not the language of responsible theological discourse at all, but of 'folk religion', with its concept of a disturbingly 'tricksy' God who nevertheless deals out substantial rewards to those who are lucky enough to please the divine fancy.

Are we to regard this last picture of God as being as authoritatively revelatory as the more sophisticated account given in the poetic sections of Job, just because it comes to us as part of the same biblical book? I do not think we can. Scripture is not uniform in its character, not only because it contains many different genres (poetry, prose, history, story, etc.) but also because of its being a human record compiled by many different people at different times in different cultural settings. Inevitably it expresses attitudes (to women, genocide and slavery, for instance) which we cannot endorse today. Inevitably, its world view is in many ways different from ours, not least because of the discoveries of science about the structure and history of the universe. Inevitably, it records all sorts of details that seem of no relevance to us today (the long lists of genealogies in 1 Chronicles 1–9, for instance). Yet having made all these necessary concessions, there remains an overall power and insight contained within the pages of the Bible to which I would certainly wish to testify. So complex and pluriform a book will be treated in complex and pluriform ways by its readers. Those of us who wish to take its revelatory potential seriously will certainly do so in a variety of ways. Nevertheless there does seem to be a sufficient general sense of the thrust of the Bible, in its testimony to the God of Israel and the God and Father of our Lord Jesus Christ, to provide a common ground on which we can meet and share our insights and our disagreements. I feel that I can discern a cousinly relationship between myself and many other Christians as we seek to bring modern knowledge and ancient experience together in a consonant combination. The endeavour affords a degree of comprehensiveness that neither source of understanding could confer on its own and that maintains a continuous connection between the wisdom of the past and the insights of the present. As I wrote in my own attempt to articulate a contemporary understanding of historic Christian faith,

> For me, the Bible is neither an inerrant account of propositional truth nor a compendium of timeless symbols, but a historically conditioned account of certain significant encounters and experiences. Read in this way, I believe it can provide the basis for a Christian belief which is certainly revised in the light of our

twentieth century insights but which is recognisably
contained within an envelope of understanding in continuity with the developing doctrines of the Church
throughout the centuries.[8]

If Judaism and Christianity were the only two world religions, there would not be much more to say. But, of course,
there are other claimed sources of revelation of the nature
of the sacred, originating from the traditions of other world
faiths, which I have not mentioned at all. These accounts are
by no means easily reconciled with the Bible or with each other
and I have already said that I am acutely aware of the difficulties that this poses for the idea that God has made the divine
nature known to humankind (chapter 2). I regard this issue as
one of the most important items on our contemporary theological agenda,[9] and I regret that I have nothing new to add on
this occasion. As a scientist I am not unacquainted with the
necessity of sometimes living with unresolved difficulties and
for the moment this is all I can do when faced with the apparent cognitive clashes of the world faiths. I do not believe
that progress would come from denying the reality of others'
religious experience or of my own Christian convictions.

8. Polkinghorne, *Belief/Faith*, p. 8.
9. Polkinghorne, *Belief/Faith*, ch. 10; *Scientists as Theologians* (SPCK, 1996),
ch. 5; *Belief in God in an Age of Science* (Yale University Press, 1998), 90–91; 111–113;
Science and Theology (SPCK, 1998), ch. 7.

CHAPTER FOUR

Design in Biology?

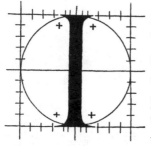 N the book of Proverbs we read, 'Three things are too wonderful for me; four I do not understand: the way of an eagle in the sky, the way of a serpent on a rock, the way of a ship on the high seas, and the way of a man with a maid' (Proverbs 30:18–19). Behind this assorted list of marvels, both natural and human, there clearly lies a feeling of awe at the world that God has made. When the Lord speaks to Job out of the whirlwind, a similar invocation is made of the mysterious wonder of creation (Job 38–41). The ancient Hebrews respected what we call nature, but they got nowhere near science. The observant gaze of the natural historian was the most that they could manage. When at length modern science came on the scene, its discoveries, particularly those revealed through the invention of the microscope, served to promote an enthusiastic appeal to an argument for the Creator's existence based on the apparent design of creation. Although this activity was often called

'physico-theology', much of the discussion was in fact biological. Philosophers such as David Hume and Immanuel Kant
might list their objections: that there were imperfections in
nature (disease and disaster); that there might have been several gods who had had a hand in the enterprise; that at best
it suggested a powerful, but not necessarily infinite, designer;
that it was all too anthropomorphic in its style. Yet, from John
Ray to William Paley and the authors of the Bridgewater Treatises (see chapter 8), the claims of this kind of natural theology were vigorously asserted and it all seemed very plausible
to many.

Charles Darwin put an end to all that. Natural selection, operating over vast tracts of time, presented an alternative understanding. The apparent products of design could,
in fact, evolve naturally without the need for the direct intervention of a divine Designer. An alternative scientific insight
had achieved what philosophical criticism had failed to do. By
the twentieth century, metabiology was no longer the happy
hunting ground of theistic argument but it had become an
atheistic waste from which the essential meaninglessness of
cosmic process would be proclaimed.[1]

Retrospectively, one can see that two theological mis-
takes had been made. One was the attempt to rival science on
the latter's own explanatory ground. We expect to use physics
to understand 'the way of a ship on the high seas'. Equally,
we should expect to use biological insights as much as we can
to understand the history of life on Earth. The second error
was to take too narrow a view of God's means of creation,
as if discontinuous decree was to be preferred to the stealthy

---

1. J. Monod, *Chance and Necessity* (Collins, 1972).

continuity of the outworking of the divinely ordained laws of nature. *Continuous* creation is a proper concept for the theologian to consider.

Theology is a complement to science and not an alternative. Accordingly, contemporary natural theologians have turned from arguments about the outcomes of natural processes to the firmer ground that is provided by consideration of the laws of nature themselves. After all, those laws are science's given starting point, but it is conceivable that they are not so self-explanatory that it is intellectually satisfying to regard them as simple brute fact. Cosmology and physics have now moved onto centre stage. Attention focusses on the Anthropic Principle's recognition of the astonishing specificity that is required of the fundamental physical laws of a universe if it is to be capable of evolving carbon-based life. Is, then, the fertility of our actual world a happy accident, or is it an indication that we are part of what is just one universe among a vast ensemble of different worlds, or is it a sign of the Creator's endowment of an inbuilt potentiality to creation? The canvassing of these different conceivable responses indicates the modest and exploratory character of contemporary thinking in natural theology.

A surprising recent development is the re-entry of some biologists into the teleological conversation. This revived discussion has been conducted at three different levels. The first of these is an extension of the kinds of argument about physical law that the physicists used in connection with uncovering the specificity of an anthropic universe. For example, one can consider the properties of water that make that remarkable fluid so necessary and effective for the development of life (at least as we know it terrestrially). A familiar instance is water's anomalous decrease of density near freezing point, which means that lakes freeze from the top downwards and so do not become huge blocks of solid ice, destroying the living creatures that are in their waters. Many other unusual aqueous properties have implications for life, for example:

(i) very high latent heats of freezing and evaporation (moderating climate change; providing an effective cooling mechanism for warm-blooded animals);

(ii) high specific heat (the oceans controlling seasonal variations of temperature within acceptable limits);

(iii) very high thermal conductivity in the liquid state (efficient heat transfer within living beings);

(iv) low thermal conductivity of ice and snow (protective insulation in cold climates);

(v) ability to dissolve almost all chemicals, at the least to a slight but detectable degree (carrying necessary minerals from the land into the sea, where life began to develop using this material).

These are just a selection of the life-supporting properties of water. More extensive discussions of the indispensable roles of water in relation to life have been given by Lawrence Henderson[2] and Michael Denton.[3] The latter goes on to give many more examples of properties of the physical world that seem 'tuned' to life's necessities. For instance, the radiation from the Sun peaks at frequencies that are just right for inducing photochemical reactions (readily facilitating photo-

2. L. J. Henderson, *The Fitness of the Environment* (Beacon Press, 1958). (First published in 1912.)

3. M. J. Denton, *Nature's Destiny* (Free Press, 1998).

synthesis and many other important biochemical processes). The absorption spectrum of the atmosphere provides a window that lets through light at these biologically useful frequencies and also (including the effects of the Earth's ozone layer) excludes harmful ultraviolet radiation. The chemistry of life is the chemistry of carbon, whose strong (covalent) chemical bonds enable the formation of the intricate molecules basic to life, with an effectiveness that is maximal at the temperatures at which water is liquid. Carbon's weak (noncovalent) chemical bonds are what generate the three-dimensional folded structures whose shapes play so vital a role in the operation of proteins and DNA in the living cell. These fruitful correlations depend upon coincidences between physical processes that appear to have no intrinsic mutual relationship. Of course, natural selection capitalises on these coincidences (photosynthesis presumably evolved in a way that made efficient use of the available energy source), but they have to be present in the physical fabric in the first place for this to be possible.

Various different kinds of argument are being deployed here. Properties of matter, such as the physical characteristics of water, derive fundamentally from the nature and strength of the electromagnetic interactions that determine the behaviour of condensed matter. Chemical bonds, similarly, are electromagnetic in origin. Arguments relating to these issues are similar to those employed by astrophysicists when they link the generation of elements within stars to the fundamental properties of nuclear forces. The only real difference is that they are somewhat less transparent in character, because of the greater difficulty in understanding details of the behaviour of complex systems such as large molecules. These properties have universal significance, for they would be the same on any planet.

In contrast, the argument relating to the matching of the Sun's radiation spectrum to atmospheric penetration and photochemical efficiency is not anchored in such generality. It is specifically environmental in character (our particular planet happens to be near a particular star). There are many other considerations of this specific kind. For example, it is thought that the possession of a large satellite (the Moon) favoured the Earth as a location for life's development through such 'useful' phenomena as the scouring action of strong tides and the stabilising effect of the Moon on the Earth's rotation. Even the existence of the massive planet Jupiter has had an effect on terrestrial life, serving to act as a partial deflector of dangerous comets and meteors, whose impacts would have had deleterious consequences. Not much significance should be attached to these fortunate aspects of our location. There are likely to be vastly many planetary systems in the universe, so it is scarcely surprising that a plethora of desirable specific conditions should be fortuitously fulfilled somewhere. (They are, however, relevant to speculations about how widespread life is in the cosmos.)

The first level of discussion, as sketched above, relates to what one might call the ground rules of the Game of Life. The second level is concerned with the question of the extent to which the actual playing of the Game may, at least to some degree, be constrained by a series of forced moves. Are the shuffling explorations of evolutionary history purely random (as neo-Darwinian theory proclaims), with survival fitness the only controlling factor, or does the story also include the effects of certain propensities that steer developments in certain pre-determined directions? Darwinian true believers are notably resistant to the suggestion that their theory might benefit from considering the possibility of augmented insight. One may suspect that metaphysical prejudgements underlie much of this resistance (radical randomness appeals to some), but it is surely a scientific question that is being posed in the first instance. In fact, there is some independent source of encouragement to take propensities seriously. Stuart Kauffman[4] has suggested that the order-generating properties of complex systems may be highly significant for biology and that many basic structures present in living creatures may be consequences of ahistorical necessity rather than the deposits of historical contingency. This claim challenges the oft-repeated assertion that every re-run of biological evolution (were that a possibility) would result in *radically* different outcomes. Of course, there is historical contingency present in what has happened, but what is being said is that this may lie more in the details than in the generality of the overall resulting patterns.[5]

Christian de Duve, who won a Nobel Prize for his work on the structural and functional organisation of the living cell, supports this point of view. He writes:

My reasons for seeing the universe as meaningful lie in what I perceive as its built-in necessities. Monod stressed the improbability of life and mind and the preponderant role of chance in their emergence, hence the lack of design in the universe, hence its absurdity and pointlessness. My reading of the same facts is differ-

4. S. A. Kauffman, *The Origins of Order* (Oxford University Press, 1993).
5. Cf. S. Conway-Morris, *The Crucible of Creation* (Oxford University Press, 1998).

ent. It gives chance the same role, but acting within such a stringent set of constraints as to produce life and mind obligatorily, not once but many times. To Monod's famous sentence 'The universe was not pregnant with life, nor the biosphere with man,' I reply: 'You are wrong. They were'.[6]

Denton is even more confident:

I believe the evidence strongly suggests that the cosmos is uniquely fit for only one type of biology—that which exists on earth—and that the phenomenon of life cannot be instantiated in any other exotic chemistry or class of material forms. Even more radically, I believe that there is a considerable amount of evidence for believing that the cosmos is uniquely fit for only one type of advanced intelligent life—beings of design and biology very similar to our own species.[7]

A number of comments should be made about this second level of the discussion of design issues in biology:

(i) No one denies a role for historical contingency. However anthropically pregnant the universe may have been, it was not uniquely destined to produce homo sapiens, in all our anatomical and physiological specificity. The strongest assertion being made by anyone is that beings *like* ourselves in complexity and capacity were a realisable potentiality, present from the start and to be expected to evolve somewhere.

(ii) Much uncertainty must inevitably attach to the claims being made, as well, of course, as to any negation of those

6. C. de Duve, *Vital Dust* (Basic Books, 1995).
7. Denton, *Destiny*, xiii.

claims. Our understanding of the nature and behaviour of complex systems is rudimentary; our insights into the pathways by which life developed on Earth are contentious and unsure; the problems involved in the full understanding of the functioning of even a single cell are immense. When Denton discusses the question of whether the terrestrial genetic code is uniquely suitable for life, he has to confess 'This is a problematical area and no clear answer can be given at present'.[8] The most one can say is that very interesting questions have been put onto the biological agenda, of a kind that might once have been supposed to have been excluded from it. The status of the discussion is very different from that involved in the physicists' contributions to the Anthropic Principle. In this latter case, all competent scientists agree on the scientific issues and it is only their further possible metaphysical consequences that are matters of controversy. For biologists, many of the scientific issues themselves remain contested.

(iii) If the authors quoted above prove in the end to have the better of the argument, what will have been attained would be the recognition of inbuilt teleological tendencies in the development of life within nature. This recognition would be compatible with a purely naturalistic account, though one enriched in its insights compared with the flat neo-Darwinian account. Of course, such striking a degree of potentiality present in the structure of the universe would also be compatible with a theistic understanding that this intrinsic fertility expressed the will of the Creator who holds the world in being and ordains its character. Indeed, it might be held to encourage such a view, though not with the force of logical neces-

8. Ibid., 161.

sity. In all metaphysical discourse, there is always the question of how far one wishes to push the search for an intellectually satisfying explanatory basis. Is it enough to rest content with the brute fact of natural law or should one look further to an Agent whose steadfast will is taken to be the basis for the perceived regularities of nature and their fruitful consequences? The authors who have been appealed to in this second level of the discussion express positive degrees of teleological belief, but they are reserved about taking explicitly the further step towards theistic interpretation. (God does not appear in Denton's index.)

The third level of the discussion is concerned with much stronger claims still. Michael Behe[9] believes that biochemistry poses problems that conventional Darwinism is incapable of solving. His central idea is that of *irreducible complexity*, which he defines as 'a single system composed of several well-matched, interacting parts that contribute to the basic function, wherein the removal of any one of the parts causes the system to effectively cease functioning'.[10] Behe describes five biological examples of what he believes are such irreducibly complex systems: the cilia that allow some cells to swim; the blood clotting system; intracellular transport of proteins; antibodies; the living synthesis of the biochemical denoted by AMP (which requires thirteen steps and involves the actions of twelve enzymes). These examples pose an evolutionary problem, for if they are correctly characterised as irreducible, their all-or-nothing, package deal character would mean that we cannot envisage their gradual, step-by-step evolution in

9. M. J. Behe, *Darwin's Black Box* (Free Press, 1996).
10. Ibid., 39.

the classical Darwinian manner. In relation to such large-scale structures as bodily organs, Darwin himself had acknowledged that 'if it could be demonstrated that any complex organ existed which could not possibly have been formed by numerous, successive, slight modifications, my theory would break down'.[11] Behe believes that he has demonstrated just such cases at the small-scale level of biochemistry and, of course, these examples, if correct, would be equally fatal to conventional Darwinism. Behe sees this as constituting evidence for what he calls 'intelligent design', meaning 'the purposeful arrangement of parts'.[12] He is cautious and reserved, however, in what he says about identifying the putative designer. The word is never spelt with a capital D and, again, God is not in the index. Yet those who have enthusiastically welcomed *Darwin's Black Box* have mostly had no such scruples. The book has been widely read as supporting a kind of creationist interventionism, involving miraculous direct divine action, rather than a gentle providential guidance exercised within the openness of natural process, of the kind that 'theistic evolutionists' tend to favour.

We have seen that the questions Behe poses are the microscopic counterparts of similar macroscopic questions asked at the time of the publication of *The Origin of Species*. Darwin himself, in his careful and scrupulous way, was troubled about how the gradual evolution of so complex and well-integrated a system as the human eye could have come about. Most present-day evolutionary theorists believe that they can suggest speculative but plausible pathways by which this might

11. Quoted, ibid.
12. Ibid., 193.

have happened. This claim is reinforced by the consideration that eyes seem to have evolved independently many times in the course of life's history. (Perhaps there has been a role here for those intrinsic structures whose existence is suggested by the insights of complexity theory.) Much less attention seems to have been given so far to the analogous problems at the biochemical level, other than in the case of the many and uncertain speculations about the origins of RNA, DNA and proteins in the first place. Behe certainly seems to raise significant issues for biologists to address but, to a by-standing physicist, it seems premature to conclude that an essential irreducibility has been firmly established.

Perhaps the most judicious conclusion about the revival of teleological issues in biology might follow along similarly cautious lines. Important and significant questions have been raised. A bleak and minimal reductionist naturalism is not the only intellectually respectable option, even at the scientific level. Theists can take heart at that, but they would be unwise, at present, to attempt to rest too strong a case on an uncertain foundation.

CHAPTER FIVE

Second Thoughts

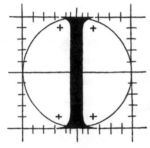NTELLECTUAL progress is usually a step-by-step process. The great geniuses may make huge leaps of creative power, but the rest of us plod along, from time to time feeling that we understand a little more than we had before. I want to offer some further remarks about issues that have been part of my thinking over many years.

5.1 CRITICAL REALISM

The idea that science succeeds in giving an increasingly verisimilitudinous account of what the physical world is like, is the fundamental belief, tacit or acknowledged, of virtually all its practitioners. It is not a belief uncontested by philosophers, for science is subtle and its method is not without a degree of intellectual precariousness.[1] Hence the belief is usually called 'critical realism', the modifying adjective being required as a recognition that scientific understanding is not just read out of nature but it is attained through a creative interpretative process. Scientist-theologians, like Ian Barbour, Arthur Peacocke, and myself, are subscribers to this belief and they find in it a basis for a cousinly relationship with theology as the latter pursues its own yet more subtle and precarious search for an understanding of the divine Reality.[2]

We have seen that one of the main defences of a critical realist position in science is based on an appeal to the actual history of scientific discovery. Although our ideas about the nature of the physical world certainly change, it is claimed that they do so in a way that suggests the attainment of an ever more accurate knowledge of a rich and many-levelled reality. I expressed such a view when I wrote,

> Scientists are mapmakers of the physical world. No map tells us all that could be said about a particular terrain, but it can faithfully represent the structure present on a certain scale. In the sense of an increasing verisimilitude, of ever better approximations to the truth of the matter, science offers us a tightening grasp of physical reality.[3]

There are many branches of science whose history is readily interpretable along these lines. The successive steps in unrav-

---

1. See J. C. Polkinghorne, *Beyond Science* (Cambridge University Press, 1996), ch. 2, for a summary of the issues. See also chapter 2 in this book.

2. See J. C. Polkinghorne, *Scientists as Theologians* (SPCK, 1996), ch. 2.

3. Polkinghorne, *Beyond Science*, 8.

elling the structure of matter—from atoms to nuclei, on to protons and neutrons, and then to quarks and gluons—seem to exhibit just such an unfolding of levels as the scale of the phenomena considered becomes smaller and smaller. If the speculations of string theory eventually prove to be correct, so that the apparently point-like quarks are themselves just states of vibration of tiny one-dimensional loops many orders of magnitude smaller than currently can be investigated, this would simply constitute a further fine-graining of our knowledge of nature.

Even the greatest revolution in the history of modern physics—the discovery of quantum theory—might be thought of as lending itself to this kind of developmental interpretation. Microscopic quantum 'fuzziness' is on too small a scale to affect the large-scale maps of macroscopic phenomena. Correspondence principles enable us to understand Newtonian mechanics as being an excellent approximate account of the behaviour of systems whose action is large on the scale set by Planck's famous constant. (One must acknowledge again that there are some unresolved perplexities about how the macroscopic and the microscopic are related to each other, of which the celebrated measurement problem is the best known.) Similarly, it is the case that Newtonian ideas can also be assimilated to those of special relativity, despite the latter's revised concepts of the nature of space, time, and simultaneity, because they can be regarded as affording 'maps' that are valid for motions where velocities are small compared to the velocity of light.

So far, so good, but the claim becomes more problematic when we turn from special relativity to general relativity, Einstein's brilliant reformulation of the theory of gravity. Newton's ideas were based on action-at-a-distance according to the inverse square law of universal gravitation. Einstein recognised that the equality of inertial mass and gravitational mass (the principle of equivalence) implied that all bodies would move in the same way in a given gravitational field. The latter could, therefore, be reinterpreted as a property of spacetime itself, related to its curvature. Effectively, Einstein replaced gravitational physics by geometry, with the equations of general relativity expressing in a beautiful and concise way how matter curves space. This transition from action-at-a-distance to geometrisation might seem to constitute, with a vengeance, a discontinuity in scientific thinking and so to offer a serious threat to a blithe assertion of critical realist continuity.

A related way of making a similar point could be framed in terms of a history of thought about the structure of the solar system. Over a two-thousand-year period, a guiding principle has been the search for mathematical elegance and simplicity in the description proposed. From Ptolemy to Copernicus, and including both, this principle was enshrined in the prime role assigned to the circle, regarded as the most perfect geometrical figure. This concept was threatened by Kepler's discovery of elliptical planetary orbits, but a new kind of mathematical beauty emerged with Newton's inverse square law, which yields the elegant consequence of equal gravitational flux through each enclosing sphere. Change came again with Einstein who discovered general relativity after an eight-year search for the most beautiful mathematical formulation of his physical ideas, now expressed in terms of the Riemannian geometry of curved space. A single guiding principle — mathematical beauty — had been found to have these three apparently quite different formulations and instantiations.

Returning to gravitational physics proper, the question is further complicated by the still-unsolved problem of how to reconcile quantum theory and general relativity with each other. Various techniques have been tried (technically ranging from quantum field theories of gravitons through string theories to 'sums over histories' of spatial geometries) without consistency being achieved. Exactly how this reconciliation will eventually modify thinking about spatial structure on the scale of the Planck length (10^{-33} cm.) is uncertain, but further revisions of a radical kind may readily be anticipated.

What are we to make of all this? Is gravitational theory the Achilles heel of critical realism, by which it can be mortally wounded? It would seem strange if this were so, given the wide range of other physical theories open to a progressive and developmental interpretation of their history. I believe that what will be found to be involved is not the abandonment of the critical realist thesis but its further sophistication. There is continuity of development, but it is located at a deeper level than is represented by those natural physical pictures that afford valuable, intuitively accessible ways of thinking about a theory (action-at-a-distance; field theory; curved space; etc.).

What is being suggested can be made clearer by considering two simple examples. The first is the figure of an ellipse. At one level this can be understood as arising through a number of different accounts of its origin, accounts that are not immediately obviously identical in their character: the curve traced out by a stick that makes taut a string attached to two fixed posts; the locus of points satisfying a certain simple equation in Cartesian geometry; the focus-directrix definition; and so on. So what, then, is an ellipse? It is, of course, not so much any one of these *particular* specifications but the reconciling mathematical reality that underlies them all.

The second example is drawn from the history of physics. In 1925, Heisenberg discovered a quantum theory expressed in terms of matrices related to properties of atomic transitions. At almost the same time, Schrödinger discovered a quantum theory expressed in terms of the dynamical properties of waves. At first, it was not at all clear that these two great discoveries were the same. It was only the deeper and more general 'transformation theory' of Dirac (who regarded this as his greatest discovery, even beyond his relativistic theory of the electron) which showed that there was only one quantum theory, capable of being articulated in a variety of forms.

Inverse square law and curved space look very different from each other and so, no doubt, will the true theory of quantum theory of gravity look very different from both of them when eventually it is discovered. Yet, I believe that there is continuity at the deep structural level (as the Schwartzchild solution shows for general relativity, as it reproduces inverse square law consequences with certain very small—and empirically successful—modifications). If this line of thinking is correct—and, of course, it will need much more detailed working out, not least in the light of further discoveries—then it has consequences for how we think about realism in science. As the trivial example of the ellipse suggests, the deep level at which verisimilitudinous development of understanding can be sought and identified is the fundamental structural level at which the mathematical notion of isomorphism operates (the same fundamental entity perceived under the cloak of a variety of descriptions). If this is a correct insight, it reinforces the claim that mathematics is indeed the natural language of physical science, the perfect medium for the expression of its insights.[4]

These considerations nudge me a little nearer to the views of my scientist-theologian colleagues, Barbour and Peacocke.[5] I have resisted the use of the concept of metaphor to describe scientific pictures of reality, for I do not see the creative ambiguity which seems part of the essence of this literary trope, as being involved in scientific description.[6] I prefer the more modest term, model. I still retain that preference, but I now acknowledge more clearly the fact that even scientific theories of wide explanatory power, such as Newton's and Einstein's gravitational theories, have in them a significant element of modelling, at least in the way in which they express their insights in terms of everyday language. This is the feature that gives rise to the possibility of apparently discontinuous change at the 'pictorial' level of description. It is, therefore, at the more abstract level of mathematical characterisation that we should seek to establish, if possible, the degree of continuity that realist claims demand. Circles are approximations to ellipses of small eccentricity. The inverse square law approximates the effects of the geometry of the Schwartzchild solution. Matrix mechanics and wave mechanics are recognised as being particular formulations of the general principles of quantum mechanics. Accounts of this kind offer the prospect of a continuing adherence to critical realism in the face of pictorial discontinuity.

4. J. C. Polkinghorne, *One World* (SPCK, 1986), 45–47.
5. See Polkinghorne, *Scientists*, 22–23.
6. J. C. Polkinghorne, *Reason and Reality* (SPCK 1991), ch. 2.

5.2 QUANTUM COSMOLOGY
AND THE ANTHROPIC PRINCIPLE

The 'fine-tuning' of the laws of nature that is necessary if the physical fabric of the world is to be capable eventually of evolving carbon-based life is an unanticipated insight first recognised by scientists in the early 1970s. There has been much discussion of its possible metascientific significance.[7] John Leslie reached a judicious conclusion when he stated that these remarkable coincidences called for some form of further explanation, whose character could take one of two different rational forms: *either* there are many different universes, each with a different set of natural laws and circumstances, and we simply live in that one where, by chance, our evolution has in fact been a possibility, *or* there is a single universe whose endowment with fruitful potentiality is the expression of the will of the Creator who has brought it into being.

If this analysis is accepted, as I think it should be, those who wish to avoid a religious conclusion will have to opt for the many-universes explanation. Their case would then be strengthened if they were able to adduce further reasons for belief in this vast portfolio of other worlds. Otherwise, it will appear simply as an ad hoc stratagem of antireligious intent. (After all, theists can point to several other reasons for their belief in God, such as the existence of cosmic order and the evidence of religious experience.)

One move in that direction stems from the recognition that the forces of nature that we observe today may well have

7. J. D. Barrow and F. J. Tipler, *The Anthropic Cosmological Principle* (Oxford University Press, 1986); J. Leslie, *Universes* (Routledge, 1989).

resulted from the spontaneous breakdown of the high symmetry that many believe was possessed by the Grand Unified Theory that held sway in the highly energetic first moments of cosmic history. This symmetry breaking need not have had a literally universal form, but there may well have been different cosmic domains in which it gave rise to different relationships between the forces effective at lower energies. Much of the anthropic discussion turns on the tight constraints that must be satisfied by these relationships (for example, between the intrinsic strengths of gravity and electromagnetism) in order for the evolution of carbon-based life to be a possibility. On this view, we simply live in that domain (greatly extended by the cosmic process of inflation) in which, by chance, things turned out 'right'.

In fact this argument, which may well be correct, only relaxes anthropic particularity to a modest degree. It would still be necessary that the initial Grand Unified Theory had the right form, both to break down to the kind of forces that we observe today and also to generate an inflationary era in very early cosmic history. In addition, the laws of quantum mechanics, which are anthropically indispensable to give the a balance between stability and openness, but which are by no means logically necessitated, would also have to be treated as given. Much would remain that is significantly special about the physical world within which we live and which had enabled it to to become our home.

It is important, therefore, to consider whether quantum cosmology might afford further help to the non-theist in the task of motivating belief in the existence of a vast variety of different universes. After all, the talk of these bold speculators seems full of reference to worlds bubbling up out of the quantum vacuum through the process of the inflationary expansion of small fluctuations. Details vary with the speaker and, in the absence of a consistent theory of quantum gravity, all such theorising is speculative and uncertain to a high degree. Yet it is not altogether inconceivable that something like these hypothesised scenarios might be a physical possibility.

The first comment to make is that any talk of quantum cosmology already assumes as its unexplained given the existence of quantum mechanics and of gravity, which are both anthropically necessary but which are by no means logically necessary properties of all possible worlds. Much, therefore, of anthropic significance has already been taken for granted before the discussion even begins. Second, the scenarios suggested are possible because the quantum vacuum is itself an active and *structured* entity. Its nature requires the specification of the quantum fields whose fluctuations are to constitute the alleged primeval chaos. In other words, just as in the case of the cosmic domain option already considered, the right Grand Unified Theory must be assumed as part of the given ground of explanation. A justly evaluated quantum cosmology, held within the bounds of bold but not altogether unmotivated scientific conjecture, in my opinion carries us little further than the better supported ideas of cosmic domains, as far as anthropic coincidences are concerned.

The appeal to quantum cosmology to avoid a theistic turn in anthropic argument has often seemed to depend upon conscious or unconscious abuse of language. 'Many-worlds' is an evocative phrase but its sober scientific use does not extend to licensing the idea of a readily realisable variety in the *basic* forms of physical law (different Grand Unified Theories). In particular, this is true of many-worlds quantum theory. Even if this interpretation of quantum mechanics were correct (which I personally do not believe to be the case), it simply supposes the existence of parallel universes in which there are different *outcomes* of quantum measurement events, and not different fundamental laws of nature.

Speculations that go beyond these limits should be clearly identified as being metascientific through and through, going beyond what can be supported by scientific knowledge or scientifically motivated conjecture. An example of this genre would be Lee Smolin's suggestion[8] that black holes spawn from within themselves new universes whose laws are slightly different from the laws of the universe containing their parent. This is an ingenious attempt to employ Darwinian explanation, so often the recourse of the reductionist, to the question of anthropic coincidences. Of course, there is no purely scientific motivation for the notion that the laws of nature would be subject to small variations in this way. The assumption is ad hoc and it is introduced solely to make a tendentious analogy with genetics. It is also alleged that there is a connection between anthropic properties and those properties that are necessary to make a universe black hole-rich. The idea then is that, because black holes spawn the 'next generation' of universes, there is a kind of supercosmic evolutionary competition in which the superior reproductive power of black hole-rich universes makes them 'fittest' in the struggle and so, by an extraordinary chance, at the same time the likelihood of the generation of anthropic universes is enhanced. In actual fact, there is considerable scientific doubt about the claim of a correlation between those properties that encourage the genera-

8. L. Smolin, *The Life of the Cosmos* (Weidenfeld and Nicholson, 1997).

tion of black holes and the fine-tuning necessary for carbon-based life[9] (which, if true, would itself be rather a remarkable coincidence).

Metaphysical stratagems of this kind have a certain air of desperation about them. The creation option has about it less sense of strain and better collateral support. It does not constitute a knockdown argument for theism but it should put that possibility on the agenda of any serious enquirer into such matters.

5.3 PANENTHEISM

Classical theism, the kind associated with the grand tradition that runs from Augustine through Aquinas and on to the Reformers and their followers, placed considerable emphasis on divine transcendence, with the concomitant assertion of a divine impassibility, invulnerable to the effects of the actions of creatures. However venerable this account may be, it is hard to reconcile its detached and distant deity with Christianity's fundamental belief that 'God is love' (1 John 4:8). Yet, for centuries the only alternative seemed to be pantheism, the theologically unacceptable equation of the Creator with creation. The trouble with this option is that it places total emphasis on absolute divine immanence, running counter to the reality of the numinous encounter with the divine Other and involving God too closely with the history of the world for there to be a credible divine Ground of hope, and Source of judgement, lying behind and beyond unfolding creaturely process.

Much theological thinking of the twentieth century has

---

9. See M. Rees, *Before the Beginning* (Simon and Schuster, 1997), 259-264.

acknowledged the unsatisfactoriness of both of these extremes and it has sought instead to find a middle ground between them. A balance is needed between transcendence and immanence. One popular way of attempting to achieve this end has been what is called panentheism, to be distinguished from pantheism by its belief that 'the Being of God includes and penetrates the whole universe, so that every part exists in Him but (as against pantheism) that his Being is more than, and is not exhausted by, the universe'.[10] Although this is a frequently quoted definition, it is by no means as transparent as one might wish and its meaning has been the subject of some dispute. To say that the being of God 'includes' the whole universe appears to imply that the cosmos is part of God, but this is qualified to an uncertain degree by the parallel word 'penetrates'. Further ambiguity is introduced when a comparison is made between the statement that the universe is 'in God' (cf. Acts 17:28), which need not carry a meaning beyond 'in the presence of', and the statement that the world does not 'exhaust' God's Being, which seems to imply that the cosmos is part of, but not the whole of, that Being.

My fellow scientist-theologians, Barbour and Peacocke, are happy to identify themselves as panentheists[11], but I have consistently declined to use that term to describe the Creator's present relationship to creation. I do, however, acknowledge that the *ultimate* destiny of creation, prefigured in the the resurrection of Christ, understood as the seed from which God's new creation has begun to grow through the redeeming transformation of the old creation, will indeed be a state in which

10. See A. R. Peacocke, *Theology for a Scientific Age*, (SCM Press, enlarged edition 1993), 371, quoting from *The Oxford Dictionary of the Christian Church*.

11. See Polkinghorne, *Scientists*, 32–33.

God is 'all in all' (1 Cor. 15:28), so I believe that panentheism will prove to be an eschatological reality.[12]

Discussion of these matters is made difficult by the delicacy of the task and the consequent difficulty of finding language adequate to express the necessary nuances. All engaged in the matter, whether panentheists or not, wish to redress classical theism's unbalanced emphasis on divine transcendence and divine invulnerability by reasserting the divine immanent presence to creation and a divine openness to sharing in creation's travail. Equally, none of us wishes to embrace a pantheistic equation of God and the world.

Some reconsideration of these issues is timely because of the publication of a careful and extensive defence of the panentheistic position by the philosopher of religion, Philip Clayton.[13] As with all panentheists, he is careful to try to maintain a distinction between Creator and creation for 'within the overarching divine presence, and even (in one sense) within the divine being itself, we remain God's created product, the work of his hands'.[14] This distinction is to be preserved by due recognition of such dichotomies as Infinite/finite and Necessary/contingent, which separate divine nature from created nature. Despite the clarity of Clayton's style, there nevertheless remain the tantalising ambiguities that seem to plague panentheistic discussion. The recurring appearance of a phrase like 'in a sense', and the uncertain import of a statement like 'we are composed, metaphorically speaking at least,

---

12. J. C. Polkinghorne, *Science and Christian Belief/The Faith of a Physicist* (SPCK 1984/Princeton University Press, 1984), 168.

13. P. Clayton, *God and Contemporary Science* (Edinburgh University Press, 1997), especially ch. 4.

14. Ibid., 90.

out of God,'[15] make it hard to be sure exactly what is being asserted. The problem of panentheistic arguments that fall short of outright assertion of divine embodiment in creation has always been to see how they represent an acceptable advance beyond classical theological thinking to which has been restored a due recognition of divine immanence.

Clayton offers a number of arguments in favour of a panentheistic position. One relates to divine omnipresence, a property that all theists would want to assert. He states with apparent approval that Newton (who had in the *Principia* described absolute space as being the *sensorium* of God) recognised that 'space must be understood also as an attribute of God, and hence as part of God'.[16] My counter to that is to appeal to the distinction made by the Orthodox between God's essence (the divine Being itself) and God's energies (God's interaction with creation). The latter are exercised within created space, and of course omnipresently, but that does not imply that space lies within the divine Being itself. It is perfectly possible to conceive of God interacting with creatures *ad extra* in a most intimate and particular fashion (perhaps, even, through active information[17]).

A second argument relates to the nature of God's absolute infinity: 'it turns out to be impossible to conceive of God as fully infinite if he is limited by something outside himself'.[18] This seems to neglect the important insight about the kenotic nature of God's creative act, which truly allows the other to

15. Ibid., 102.
16. Ibid., 89.
17. J. C. Polkinghorne, *Belief in God in an Age of Science* (Yale University Press, 1998), ch. 3.
18. Ibid., 99.

be, as a gracious act of divine withdrawal and self-limitation. This qualification of absolute infinity is freely granted by the Creator and not exacted by the creature. Panentheism, in this mode of argument, is in danger of replacing classical theology's unsatisfactory notion of God's absolute power by an equally unsatisfactory notion of God's absolute comprehensiveness.

A third argument relates to causality. Clayton conceives of God's providential and sustaining relationship with creation along the lines of what he calls the 'panentheistic analogy',[19] exploiting a claimed comparison with human embodied experience. This might seem to amount to a discreetly diluted appeal to divine embodiment. There are other ways of avoiding unacceptable notions of fitful divine intervention by recourse to alternative analogies suggestive of continuous interaction, without having to appeal to this highly dubious idea (see chapter 6).

A fourth argument relates to the closeness of God's relationship to creation. It is certainly true that 'panentheism conceives of an ontologically closer relationship between God and humanity than has traditionally been asserted',[20] but a strengthened conception of divine immanence is all that is really needed for this desirable end. This can be achieved without recourse to panentheism, by taking more seriously God's presence to creation.

Clayton appeals for support to the writings of one of the leading theologians of the second half of the twentieth century, Jürgen Moltmann. Because Moltmann is a creative theo-

---

19. Ibid., 101.
20. Ibid., 102.

logical thinker, rather than a cool philosophical writer, there can be a number of opinions about exactly how panentheistic his thinking actually is. He has certainly powerfully expressed the idea of a kenosis involved in the divine act of creation. When discussing how God can bring into being an 'external' reality, he says 'it is only the assumption of a self-limitation by God himself preceding his creation which can be reconciled with God's divinity without contradiction'.[21] Moltmann uses the kabbalistic notion of *zimsum* (a divine making way) to explore this concept. He can say that 'God makes room for his creation by withdrawing his presence,'[22] but he can also say 'if creation *ad extra* takes place in the space freed by God himself, then in this case the reality outside God still remains *in* the God who has yielded up that 'outwards' in himself'.[23] The matter is further complicated by the fact that Moltmann, one of the 'theologians of hope', is strongly eschatological in his thinking, locating ultimate significance in the fulfilment of God's future. He speaks of 'The movement from God's initial self-limitation to his eschatological delimitation'.[24] For Moltmann, the cross and the resurrection are the key to God's nature and purpose: 'In the path of the Son into self-emptying and bondage, to the point of the death he died, and in the path of his exaltation and glorification by the whole creation, God *becomes* omnipresent'[25] (my italics). I have already indicated my belief in an eschatological panentheism.

I remain of the opinion that God's caring relationship

21. J. Moltmann, *God in Creation* (SCM Press, 1985), 86.
22. Ibid., 87.
23. Ibid., 88–89.
24. Ibid., 89.
25. Ibid., 91.

with creation is best understood in terms of a divine immanent presence, hiddenly active in a universe which is allowed to be itself through the gracious act of God's self-limited allowing of the existence given to this other. A useful phrase (for which I am indebted to Fraser Watts) is that creation is within the *life* of God, which carries with it overtones of the Orthodox concept of the active presence of divine energies. In my view, panentheistic language is best reserved to express eschatological destiny rather than to describe present reality.

5.4 DUAL ASPECT MONISM

The classical metaphysical strategies of materialism, idealism and Cartesian dualism all exhibit a bankruptcy in the face of the many-layered, and yet interconnected, character of our encounter with reality. This recognition encourages the search for some form of dual aspect monism, an account that would acknowledge the fundamental distinction between experience of the material and experience of the mental but which would neither impose on reality a sharp division into two unconnected kinds of substance nor deny the psychosomatic unity of human beings. Stating this metaphysical aspiration is one thing; its attainment, even in a sketchy and conjectural form, is quite another. I have from time to time tentatively explored the suggestion that the notion of complementarity, derived by analogy from quantum theory but clearly being employed in a different context and so, necessarily, in a novel manner, might afford a way of thinking about these issues.[26] If that is the case, an analogy with quantum

26. J. C. Polkinghorne, *Science and Creation* (SPCK 1988), ch. 5; *Reason*, ch. 3; *Belief/Faith*, ch. 1; *Belief in God*, ch. 3.

field theory (which perfectly resolves the apparent paradox of wave/particle duality) would suggest that the presence of a degree of indefiniteness in the scientific account of dynamical process might be an important ingredient in facilitating a subtle and supple metaphysics, by analogy with the way in which states with an indefinite number of particles can manifest wavelike properties. This idea has encouraged me in the realist strategy of interpreting the intrinsic unpredictabilities that are found in modern physics as signs of an openness of physical process to the future, so that what might have seemed to be unfortunate epistemological deficiencies are reinterpreted as fortunate ontological opportunities.

One of the most promising developments that one may foresee lies in an increasingly insightful study of complex systems. Previously the best that could be done to understand their behaviour was some sort of averaging procedure, such as that employed in statistical mechanics. The advent of high-speed computing has enabled much more detailed work to be done on specific models. At present, the subject of complexity theory is at the natural history stage of studying exemplary 'for instances'. The deeper general theory, of whose existence there are clear hints in surprising emergences of regularities and patterns of order, is currently unknown.

Undoubtedly big discoveries lie ahead. It is already clear, from the role of strange attractors in chaos theory and from the spontaneous generation of long-range order in dissipative systems far from thermal equilibrium that, in addition to traditional descriptions in terms of matter and energy, there is a need to introduce a third fundamental concept of a pattern-forming character that will embrace these emergent properties of holistic order. Information might be a suitable word for it. It carries with it just a *glimmer* (no more) of the integration of the material with something that begins to look a little like the mental. Just as relativity theory has integrated matter and energy into a single account, so one might hope for an eventual discovery (at least as revolutionary as relativity, and most probably much more so) that would integrate the triad: matter-energy-information. That achievement would be a significant step in the search for a dual aspect monism.

It would, however, be no more than a first move in a direction whose ultimate goal was still over the horizon. A much more important step would have been made if it were ever possible to attain an understanding in which consciousness was taken into an integrated account. Despite many over-confident reductionist claims to the contrary, consciousness is presently both an undeniable experience and also an irreducible mystery. Neuroscientists may utter slogans such as 'the mind is synaptic', but the truth is that all their important and successful efforts to study neural pathways in the brain still leave us unable to bridge the gap that yawns between that kind of talk and the simplest mental experiences of seeing blue or feeling thirsty.

If a dual aspect monism is on the right track, then there will be entities, such as stones, whose nature is located wholly at the material pole, and other entities, such as ourselves, who are 'amphibians', participating in both kinds of polar experience. It would seem entirely reasonable to suppose that there are also entities whose nature is located wholly at the mental pole. (This could provide a metaphysical lodging place for created non-embodied spiritual beings, such as angels, if such there are.) There is another candidate for this end of the metaphysical spectrum, less controversial than angels, namely, the truths of mathematics. There is a widespread conviction among mathematicians (which I share[27]) that the pursuit of their subject involves discovery and not mere construction. Mathematical entities, such as the prime numbers and the Mandelbrot set, are 'out there' in some platonic world of mathematical ideas. Not only can a dual aspect monism accommodate such a belief but also this conviction of the mathematicians would point to an interesting aspect of such a metaphysics.

The material world is a world of process, characterised by temporality and becoming. Theologically this means, as Augustine knew, that the physical universe was created *cum tempore*, with time itself a created entity (a point of view fully compatible with modern relativity theory's integration of space, time and matter). A noetic world containing the truths of mathematics would have a different character. It would be everlasting, in the sense that such truths just *are* and do not evolve. We can think of such a world as being part of creation, but it has 'always' been in the rational Mind of God. It follows then that, if these two worlds, material and noetic, are but complementary aspects of a larger created reality, then the duality involved in that wider picture is more than just that of material/mental; it must also embrace becoming/being and everlasting/temporal. Once again, humanity is the 'great amphibian', participating in both poles of this complex reality. We are creatures of time, but we also have intuitions of a reality beyond change and flux. One sees that in the pursuit of a fully integrated metaphysics, the multiplicity of experience leads us to an account of considerable richness and subtlety.

27. Polkinghorne, *Belief in God*, ch. 6.

One final point remains. This discussion has been concerned with a tentative metaphysical account of created reality. The divine Reality has been outside the scope of our discussion. Yet it has been a repeated theme in much twentieth century theological thinking that, by an act of divine condescension, the Creator has also embraced a duality of Being and becoming within the divine nature itself, so that the Eternal, who is beyond time, is also the God of history who acts within time.[28]

5.5 CHAOS THEORY

This is not so much a case of second thoughts as of nth thoughts, for I have frequently written on this topic.[29] Partly that has been a process of clarifying my own thoughts and partly it has been a response to what seems to me to have been some persistent misunderstandings on the part of my critics. I want to indicate what I believe to be the fundamental points at issue between us.

First, let me state the obvious fact that there is no entailment possible from physics to metaphysics, though there is a degree of constraint. Epistemology (in this case, unpredictability) does not determine ontology (in this case, the question of the nature of causal process). Metaphysical questions must receive metaphysical answers that are given for metaphysical reasons. I have repeatedly sought to explain the meta-

28. See, for example, J. C. Polkinghorne, *Science and Providence* (SPCK, 1989), ch. 7.

29. Cf. footnote 25 and J. C. Polkinghorne, 'The Metaphysics of Divine Action' in R. J. Russell, N. Murphy and A. R. Peacocke (eds.), *Chaos and Complexity* (Vatican Observatory, 1995), 147–156.

physical motivations that lie behind my own position. What I wish to reassert is that, in making a metaphysical conjecture, I am acting no differently from anyone else who seeks to speak on questions of causality and agency. Some of my critics seem to suppose that by invoking the admittedly widely held view that quantum measurement events are indeterminate in outcome, they are adopting a position of metaphysical privilege that dispenses them from the precariousness of conjecture. Acquaintance with the philosophy of quantum theory soon disabuses one of this notion. All of us, without exception, have to make metaphysical guesses. I am certainly not against the exploration of a multitude of approaches to the difficult issue of agency. I simply want to argue for a fair account of what is involved in arguing for *any* of these approaches.

Second, chaos theory identifies the existence of exquisitely sensitive systems whose future behaviour is intrinsically unpredictable. This is the epistemological base from which all of us must start who wish to explore the possibilities offered to metaphysics by this unexpected physical behaviour. To describe chaos theory as concerned with 'non-linear dynamics', whose equations are to be solved in a space of integrable (well-behaved) functions,[30] *is already to have opted for a particular metaphysical interpretation of the nature of such systems.* If that description is accepted, then we do indeed have 'deterministic chaos', so that we would be concerned with unavoidable ignorance and not with an openness of process to the future. It is not, however, in any logical sense a necessity to adopt this point of view. I have repeatedly emphasised that there is the alternative of interpreting the non-linear equations, whose

30. See I. Prigogine, *The End of Certainty* (Free Press, 1997).

computer-generated solutions led to the discovery of chaos, as approximations, in the limit case of separability, to a more subtle, supple and holistic account of physical reality.

Third and finally, let me stress once more the *holistic* character of top-down active information. It is a complete misrepresentation of my ideas to suggest that they imply that agency arises from the local manipulation of either boundary conditions or microscopic processes, either by humans or by God.

Part II

DIVINE AGENCY

CHAPTER SIX

God in Relation to Nature: Kenotic Creation and Divine Action

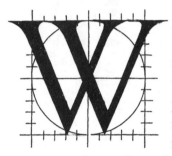HATEVER it may mean to say that God is personal, such language must surely imply that God is active, doing particular things on particular occasions and not just functioning as an unchanging effect like the law of gravity. In recent years, the intellectual conversation between science and theology has moved from natural theology's appeal to God as the ground of order and fruitfulness, to a more central theistic concern with the God of providence. On the one hand, we have science's account of the regularity of the processes of nature. On the other hand, we have Christian theology's claim to speak of the God who acts in history. Can the two be reconciled with each other? Achieving this end may require some flexibility from both science and theology in their assessments of the understandings that they bring to the dialogue.

The philosopher of history and historian of ideas, R. G.

Collingwood, in his posthumously published book, *The Idea of Nature*,[1] proposed the thesis that there have been three eras in reflective thinking about the nature of the world, corresponding respectively to: (i) the ancient Greeks and their medieval intellectual successors; (ii) the Renaissance period and the birth of modern science; (iii) the modern period of the past two hundred years. In the first era, nature was thought of on the model of an organism. Greek natural science, Collingwood tells us, 'was based on the principle that the world of nature is saturated or permeated by mind'.[2] Its ceaseless motion arises from its being alive. In the second era, nature was thought of on the model of a machine. The physical world was considered to be clockwork so that, in the thought of Descartes, even animals were treated as being merely intricate robots. The only exception to this rule was the intentional acts willed by human minds or by disembodied spirits. Notoriously, Cartesian metaphysics proved impotent to integrate, in a satisfactory manner, mental acts with the motion of extended matter. Collingwood believed that what distinguished the modern era from its two predecessors was the recognition of the role of history. Thus unfolding process, particularly evolutionary process, is the fundamental model in its thinking about nature.

Such tidy schemes can be produced only by a somewhat coarse-grained account that does not worry much about contrary details. More refined analysis will reveal the ebb and flow of currents and counter-currents of opinion.[3] Never-

---

1. R. G. Collingwood, *The Idea of Nature* (Oxford University Press, 1945).
2. Ibid., 3.
3. See C. Kaiser, *Creation and the History of Science* (Marshall Pickering, 1991) for a more complex account.

theless, Collingwood's broad-brush classification provides a useful framework for metaphysical thinking. Nature may be considered either as being in some sense alive, or as being mechanical, or as an unfolding process bringing emergent novelty into being.

Just as physics does not determine metaphysics, though it certainly constrains it, so metaphysics in its turn does not determine theology, though it certainly constrains the kind of theological thinking that will seem congenial and convincing. Each of Collingwood's three options has associated with it a particular way of conceiving of God and of God's relationship to nature.

If the world were an organism, then it would be natural to think of God in terms of the World Soul. Divine action with respect to the universe might then be expected to be analogous to our human action within our bodies. A few contemporary theologians, such as Grace Jantzen,[4] explicitly defend the idea of divine embodiment in the world. In addition, the idea of nature as an organism is a commonplace of much New Age thinking, usually expressed in the parochial terms of terrestrial Gaia rather than those of a truly cosmic Ouranos.

Scientifically, such ideas founder because, however integrated Earth's ecosystem may or may not prove to be, the universe itself is too disseminated an entity to be described convincingly in organic terms. It does not possess anything like the elaborate degree of causal inter-relationships that characterises the parts of an organism.

Metaphysically, such ideas founder because, if they are not to amount to a simple pantheistic equation of nature and

4. G. Jantzen, *God's World, God's Body* (Darton, Longman and Todd, 1984).

God, their implementation requires reliance on the dubious dualistic notion of a distinct separation between the soul (mirroring God) and the body (mirroring the universe).

Theologically, such ideas founder because they bind God too closely to creation, making divine existence coextensive with that of the universe, so that it is presumably finite in the past (beginning with the big bang) and, perhaps, finite in the future also (ending with the big crunch). God would then die with the death of the cosmos. So total a degree of divine immanence is theologically unacceptable, for it would imply that God is in thrall to the history of the universe.

The concept could, however, be modified in a number of ways. Panentheism retains the ghost of divine embodiment in its belief that 'the Being of God includes and penetrates the whole universe, so that every part of it exists in Him but (as against pantheism) that His Being is more than, and is not exhausted by, the universe'.[5] Arthur Peacocke denies that this implies that the world is in some sense a part of God,[6] but doubts must linger about whether this particular way of seeking to maintain a balance between divine transcendence and divine immanence can succeed in the delicate feat of avoiding such a conclusion. Certainly the doyen of panentheists, Charles Hartshorne, said that God 'is both the system [the universe] and something independent of it'[7] (see also, chapter 5.3).

The highly speculative and uncertain ideas of quantum

---

5. *The Oxford Dictionary of the Christian Church*; quoted with approval by A. R. Peacocke, *Theology for a Scientific Age* (SCM Press, 1993), 371.

6. Peacocke, ibid.

7. C. Hartshorne, *The Divine Relativity* (Yale University Press, 1948), 90.

cosmology[8] could provide a way of rescuing such a God from sharing the fate of our observable universe. According to some theories, this world is just one among infinitely many that bubble up out of a universal and truly active medium, the vacuum state of quantum gravity. Each individual world rises and falls, but the process itself continues ceaselessly 'for ever'. If there is room for a God in such speculations, it might seem to lie in a pantheistic identification of the divine with the quantum vacuum itself, an idea of extreme theological etiolation.

If the world were a mechanism, then it would be natural to think of God as the Celestial Engineer. Divine action would be limited to the initial construction, and the subsequent maintenance in existence, of the cosmic machine. Perhaps there might also be a need for occasional interventions to correct faulty workings, were they to occur. This is the kind of view that Isaac Newton seems to have held, at least about the non-human universe, believing that tendencies to instabilities in the solar system would require divine attention every fifty thousand years or so if the system's integrity were to be maintained. Newton was deeply impressed by the beautiful and orderly construction of the celestial machine, claiming that this demonstrated that there must be divine Intelligence behind its contrivance. However, such an interpretation proved not to provide lasting intellectual satisfaction. Leibniz was quick to point out that a machine that required periodic attention to keep it going fell short of the perfection expected of divine handiwork. Worse still, once God had been reduced

---

8. See R. J. Russell, N. Murphy and C. J. Isham (eds.), *Quantum Cosmology and the Laws of Nature* (Vatican Observatory, 1993).

to being just a clockmaker, the apparent self-sufficiency of the machine threatened to make otiose even that deistic role. This was to lead later in the eighteenth century to the atheistic proclamation of the properties of matter as being the sole and sufficient ground of explanation. In many minds, God seemed to have been made redundant.

Scientifically, such ideas founder on the twentieth-century discoveries of quantum theory and chaos theory. The widespread intrinsic unpredictabilities that these theories entail show that the physical world is not simply mechanical, in the sense of being predictable and controllable, but it is something subtler, and perhaps suppler, than that.

Metaphysically, such ideas founder on their inability, in any convincing way, to accommodate mental activity within their account of reality. We should not so readily abandon the attempt to take seriously that realm of experience which, in actual fact, is the ground of all our perception and knowledge.

Theologically, such ideas founder not only because the God of deism is inadequate to account for the Christian intuitions of prayer and providence but also because, as we have seen, God has so little to do that, for many, a thorough-going atheism eventually appears to be a more economical proposition. At best, the question of divine existence is left open, its answer laden with so little consequence that it becomes almost a matter of indifference what that answer might prove to be.

If the world is an evolving process still *in via*, then God may be expected to be in interactive relationship with its unfolding history. There is no need, however, for the Creator to be a Cosmic Tyrant, in total control of all that is happening. Indeed, the play of creation, as we perceive it, has more the appearance of an improvisation than the appearance of the performance of a predetermined script. Recall that one of the immediate Christian responses to the publication in 1859 of Charles Darwin's *Origin of Species* was Charles Kingsley's recognition that the Creator was no longer to be thought of as the originator of a ready-made world but as the giver of a creation 'allowed to make itself'. In twentieth-century theology, this idea has been developed to the point of acknowledging that there is a divine kenosis involved in the act of creation. The Creator self-limits divine power in allowing the created-other to be truly itself, in its God-given freedom of being. Such a degree of setting aside of total divine control is perceived to be fitting for the God whose character is love and whose nature would be incompatible with the exercise of a cosmic tyranny. A kenotic account of creation is of great significance in theodicy's attempt to wrestle with the perplexities posed by the evil and suffering so clearly and painfully present in the world. If it is the case that not every event is brought about by a direct exercise of divine power, then not everything that happens can be expected to accord with God's benevolent will. Just as the human exercise of free will can lead either to the deeds of a Mother Teresa or to the deeds of a Stalin, so nature allowed to make itself will be a world in which death is the necessary cost of new life, the possibility of genetic mutations producing new species cannot be divorced from the possibility of genetic mutations producing malignancy, rain for crops and destructive storm winds will both form part of the way the weather turns out to be. Among theologians who have particularly developed this theme has been Jürgen Moltmann[9] (em-

9. J. Moltmann, *The Trinity and the Kingdom of God* (SCM Press, 1981), ch. 4; *God in Creation* (SCM Press, 1985), ch. 4.

ploying the kabbalistic notion of *zimsum*, a divine ontological making-room for the existence of another) and W. H. Vanstone [10] (based on a meditative consideration of the necessary precariousness involved in any loving act of creativity and on a recognition of the value conferred by such an act). Scientifically, such ideas draw support from two kinds of discovery that have been made in the past two centuries.

The first set relates to an increasing acknowledgement of the role of historical process in the formation of the physical world as we observe it today: successively the discovery, in the late eighteenth and early nineteenth centuries, of the geological history of the Earth; the recognition, in the late nineteenth century, of the evolving biological history of life on Earth; the discovery, somewhat reluctantly arrived at in the early twentieth century, that the universe itself has had a history, stemming from the big bang.

The second set is the discovery of intrinsic unpredictabilities, of the kind already referred to, in the behaviour of both quantum mechanical and classical physical systems. If these phenomena are to be understood as signs of the openness of the future to the emergence of true novelty, then their unpredictabilities will have to be interpreted, not just as epistemological defects, limiting our ability to know in detail what is going to happen, but as ontological opportunities, permitting the operation of additional causal principles, over and above the energetic transactions that physics describes.

In the case of quantum theory, such a strategy has been

10. W. H. Vanstone, *Love's Endeavour, Love's Expense* (Darton, Longman and Todd, 1977).

almost universally adopted, so that, in the minds of most physicists, Heisenberg's uncertainty principle has become a principle of *indeterminacy*. The additional causal principle held to be operating in this case is then usually considered to be pure randomness, so that the outcomes of indeterminate quantum measurements are said to occur simply 'by chance'.

In the case of chaos theory, this ontological option has been far less popular, though it has been defended by some people, including the present writer.[11] What the corresponding additional causal principles might be will be discussed shortly. The philosophical case for treating quantum theory and chaos theory similarly in this respect derives from the fact that what would then be involved for either theory would be an alignment of epistemology (knowledge of future behaviour limited by intrinsic unpredictability) and ontology (the claim of a corresponding causal openness) as closely as possible with each other. This strategy would accord well with the realist stance adopted, consciously or unconsciously, by scientists in relation to the significance of their work. Contrary to Kant, they do not divorce *phenomena* (known appearance) from *noumena* (the real nature of things). Unless one were learning, by means of science's intricate and artificially contrived experimental procedures, what the world is really like, the whole enterprise would not seem worth the time, talent and treasure spent upon it. A critical realist interpretation of this kind is not logically necessary, either for quantum theory or for chaos

---

11. I. Prigogine, *The End of Certainty* (Free Press, 1996); for a recent summary of my thinking, see J. C. Polkinghorne, *Belief in God in an Age of Science* (Yale University Press, 1998), ch. 3.

theory, but it is needed to sustain the scientific endeavour and, I would claim, to explain its success.[12]

Metaphysically, such ideas draw their support from the consideration that an extension of causal principles beyond the energetic exchanges described by a reductionist physics, might offer the glimmer of the possibility of accommodating, within this enhanced understanding, a genuinely instrumental role for mind, active in the execution of human intentions. Whether this hope has any grounds is a question that we looked at briefly in chapter 5.4.

Theologically, such ideas draw support from the related consideration that a physical world found to be sufficiently supple in its process to accommodate human agency, might also be expected to display an analogous ability to be open to divine providential action. Although the possibility of this prospect has certain obvious attractions for the theologian, it also represents embarking on a line of argument that runs counter to much traditional theological thinking. Its frank appeal to an analogy between human and divine agency might seem to lead to the danger of assimilating the Creator to creatures, an elision that the classical Judaeo-Christian-Islamic tradition has always strenuously resisted, believing that God must remain God, in all the uniqueness and ineffability of deity.

A further danger might be feared to lie in the appeal being made to twentieth-century science. Dean Inge warned us that he who marries the spirit of the age will soon find himself a widower. The history of science is full of revisions—of

---

12. For a summary, see J. C. Polkinghorne, *Scientists as Theologians* (SPCK, 1996) ch. 2. See also the discussion in chapter 2 of this volume.

revolutions, even, if we were to credit the account of Thomas Kuhn.[13] In any case, are we to suppose that, before the discoveries of quantum theory and chaos theory, an honest theologian was impotent to talk convincingly of God's action in the world? That is certainly not how the record of theological tradition actually reads. Many of its most influential figures used an altogether different metaphysical strategy for their discussion of providence.

Classical Christian theology from Augustine onwards, and most powerfully expressed in the writings of Aquinas, sought to preserve the uniqueness of divine action by speaking of God's primary causality, exercised in and under the manifold secondary causalities of creatures. No explanation was given of how this happens; it was simply said to be the case. Any attempt to exhibit the 'causal joint' by which the double agency of divine and creaturely causalities related to each other was held to be impossible, or even impious. Three assertions were important consequences of this point of view.

The first was that the ineffability of the mode of action of this primary causality had the effect of totally repudiating any possibility of an analogy between human and divine agencies.

A second assertion was that God is fully party to every event, not simply by allowing it to happen by divine permission as the creation is held in being, but in bringing it about through the exercise of divine will. Nothing is outside direct divine control, an assertion that poses obvious problems for theodicy, which can only match the veiled and mysterious character of primary causality with the veiled and mysterious

13. T. Kuhn, *The Structure of Scientific Revolutions* (University of Chicago Press, 1970).

claim that in the end all will be found to have been for the best. *O felix culpa!* is to be written over all of human, terrestrial and cosmic history.

The third assertion was that primary causality is so divorced in character from secondary causality that it may be held to be active whatever form the latter is believed by science to take. Theology is made invulnerable to whatever may currently be claimed about the process of the physical world. It seems that this feature has had a particular attraction for twentieth-century defenders of primary causality, such as Austin Farrer.[14] However, some of us feel that the deep obscurity involved in the idea of a double agency, operating simultaneously through both primary causality and secondary causalities, carries with it the danger that the discussion might turn out to be no more than double talk.

What, for its partisans, is the strength of the idea of primary and secondary causality is, for its critics, its greatest weakness. The strategy represents an extreme case of a 'two-languages' approach to understanding how theology and science relate to each other. Their discussions are treated as independent, so that they talk past each other at different levels of discourse. The two disciplines might then be considered as presenting two different paradigms or involving participation in two different language games. This is a point of view that is rightly emphatically rejected by many who work at the interface between science and theology, and particularly by such scientist-theologians as Barbour, Peacocke and myself.[15] In its place, we wish to assert that the unity of knowl-

---

14. A. Farrer, *Faith and Speculation* (A&C Black, 1967).
15. See Polkinghorne, *Scientists*, ch. 1.

edge and truth—a unity ultimately guaranteed by the oneness of the Creator—means that there is active intercourse across the boundary between the two disciplines, of a kind variously characterised as aiming at consonance, dialogue, integration, or assimilation. In our view, creation is not so distanced from its Creator that the character of its history and process affords no clue to the nature of God's interaction with it.

Those who adopt this latter stance then have to explain how they are to understand and cope with the changes that occur in scientific understanding and how these might relate to theology. Broadly speaking, the answer will be the same beyond science as it is within it. The clue lies in the recognition both of the limited and provisional character of current knowledge and also of the persistence of some well-tested forms of insight beyond the era of their discovery. Contemporary science is always incomplete but it is also the platform from which the continuing search for a fuller and more secure understanding can be launched. At any given time, current science will include some elements that will prove long-lasting and some in need of correction. There will also be some phenomena that are known to occur but whose nature is still beyond the reach of current theory. In other words, science is both precarious and successful, requiring a humble assessment of its achievements but yielding lasting insights and rewarding boldness in their further exploitation and extension.

Galileo provides an example of what I mean. He began to develop a recognisably modern and successful concept of inertia in order to explain how the Earth could be rotating on its axis and encircling the Sun, without our being aware of this in terms of obvious terrestrial phenomena (such as would have been the case if we had been left behind!). This was an immensely important insight of lasting validity. At the same time, he believed that these ideas could also be used to explain the action of the tides and he repudiated Kepler's suggestion that the Moon might play an important role in this phenomenon. In this respect, Galileo was mistaken, as soon became apparent. Neither he nor Kepler could make quantitative progress in understanding the details of tidal behaviour. That required Newton's great discovery of the existence of universal gravity and the precise form that it took. Yet Newton, as he said, 'stood on the shoulders of giants' and his theory of motion built on the insights of Galileo. This story of partial and provisional success leading on to further advance, is characteristic of the way that science progresses, bit by bit. Some of its ideas will prove transient but some of them will prove enduring.

Many phenomena have become known to science well before a theoretical framework was in place for understanding them. At the end of the nineteenth century, physicists could not reconcile the temperature of the Earth, or the continued shining of the Sun, with the long periods of time over which the evolutionary biologists asserted that these phenomena must have been sustained. Radioactivity (which generates heat within the Earth) and nuclear reactions (which fuel the Sun) were then unknown and unsuspected. Lord Kelvin was rash enough to claim that the physicists' inability to comprehend these long-lasting phenomena must mean that the biologists were mistaken. The error, however, was Kelvin's and it derived from his overconfidence about the completeness of nineteenth-century physics. Later, many properties of matter and of radiation became known which remained unintelligible until the discovery of quantum theory shed light on the processes that lay behind them.

Almost all scientists believe the progress of science to be a convergence onto an increasingly verisimilitudinous understanding of the nature of the physical world. We are its mapmakers and sometimes we have radically to revise our views (that patch of apparent Newtonian terra firma turns out to be a quantum swamp). Yet overall, accuracy improves with each major discovery. Scientific progress is not made either by denying the existence of phenomena that we currently cannot understand or by exaggerating (as the elderly Kelvin did) the scope of what we have currently achieved. Persistence and openness in investigation, and a degree of realistically humble assessment of present attainment, are indispensable virtues in the pursuit of science.

This edifying conclusion is of wider application than just within science alone. It certainly bears extension to theology and to the interaction between theology and science. If we do not display a certain degree of intellectual daring, no progress will be made. If we do not display a certain degree of intellectual humility, misleading and untenable claims will be made. If we are not content to live with the acknowledgement that there are phenomena that are beyond our contemporary powers of explanation, we shall have a truncated and inadequate grasp of reality.

Human agency, and divine providential agency, both clearly fall into the category of experience that is presently beyond our capacity for full understanding. As persons, we should not deny our basic experience of free choice and consequent moral responsibility. Nor should we deny our experiences of prayer and intimations of providence. As Christians, we should hold fast to our intuition, and the testimony of our tradition, that God acts in the world. As rational thinkers convinced of the unity of knowledge, we should not forgo the attempt, however modest and tentative it must necessarily be, to see whether a metaphysical conjecture, based on an ontological interpretation of the intrinsic unpredictabilities of physical process, might not afford us some insight into questions of agency. That is the task to which we must now return.

One of the first attempts of this kind was made by William Pollard,[16] who looked to the uncertainties of quantum events to provide some room for providential manoeuvre. The idea has been revived by a number of writers[17] but this approach encounters some difficulties. One is that quantum events take place in the atomic realm of the very small and the resulting uncertainties tend to cancel each other out when a very large number of such events are combined to describe the behaviour of a lump of matter of a size sufficient to be relevant to what is happening on a humanly perceptible and significant scale. Another problem is that quantum uncertainties relate only to those particular kinds of events that we call measurements, by which is meant irreversible macroscopic registration of a state of affairs, and not simply conscious observation. By its nature, measurement only occurs from time to time, so that agency exercised in this way would have a curiously sporadic character. Finally, we may observe that if microscopic quantum events are to have macroscopic consequences, this can only be through an enhancement of their effect due to their being part of a much larger system which is extremely sensitive to

16. W. G. Pollard, *Chance and Providence* (Faber & Faber, 1958).

17. See R. J. Russell, N. Murphy and A. R. Peacocke (eds.), *Chaos and Complexity* (Vatican Observatory, 1995), articles by N. Murphy and T. F. Tracy; R. J. Russell, W. R. Stoeger and F. J. Ayala, *Evolutionary and Molecular Biology* (Vatican Observatory, 1999), article by R. J. Russell.

the fine details of its circumstance. Chaotic systems have this character (though it is necessary to add that currently there is a degree of perplexity about how to think correctly about the mutual relationship of microscopic quantum systems and macroscopic chaotic systems). For these reasons, the primary focus of our discussion will be on the possibilities offered directly by chaotic unpredictabilities.

We have seen that if these unpredictabilities are to be given an ontological interpretation, this will imply that additional causal principles must be at work bringing about the future, over and above the effect of the energetic exchanges between constituents which conventional physics describes. Although there is currently no fully articulated theory of these extra causal principles, their general character is fairly clear.

Study of complex systems has served to emphasise that our description of physical process must have a dual character, involving not only energy but also what one might call 'pattern'. The future behaviour of a chaotic system is not totally haphazard. It displays a kind of orderly disorder. What will happen is confined within a large but restricted range of possibilities that technically is called a 'strange attractor'. This consists of a portfolio of possible future patterns of motion, all of the same energy but differing in the details of the way in which they unfold. There are a number of executive toys consisting of jointed rods and weights which, when released from apparently the same configuration, nevertheless exhibit a bewildering and unpredictable variety of subsequent motions. Playing with one of these toys is just an exploration of its strange attractor. The openness that a chaotic system can be interpreted as possessing corresponds to the multiplicity of possibilities contained within this strange attractor, and any one of the motions that is actually executed can be understood as corresponding to an expression of the information specifying its detailed structure ('this way, then that way, etc.').

The corresponding new causal principles can, therefore, be anticipated to complement energetic causality with a pattern-forming informational causality. This conjecture is reinforced by considering other recent discoveries. Dissipative systems, maintained far from thermodynamic equilibrium by the input of energy from their environment, can manifest the spontaneous generation of an astonishing degree of orderly pattern. For example, in a certain type of convective fluid motion between two heated plates, the movement is confined within a regular series of hexagonal convection columns, an effect involving the correlated motion of trillions of molecules. Complex systems manifest surprising powers of self-organisation. For example, computer simulations of networks of lights, whose switching on and off is linked in a certain simple way to the state of their neighbours, are found spontaneously to settle down to a limited number of orderly patterns of behaviour, rather than continuing to flash haphazardly for ever. A system of this kind with 10,000 bulbs would have about 10^{3000} different possible states, but its behaviour soon converges upon about 100 of them. This constitutes the self-generation of an amazing degree of orderliness.

A second feature of chaotic systems is that they are un-isolatable. Because they are so sensitive, they can never be insulated from the effect of the environment in which they are located. Therefore they must be discussed holistically, in their total overall context.

Putting these two insights together, we can see that in an

ontological approach to interpreting chaos theory, one would expect there to be additional causal principles of an holistic and pattern-forming kind. One might, in brief, call such a causality 'active information' and denote its holistic character by the phrase 'top-down causality', meaning by that the influence of the whole upon its parts. In somewhat differing ways, Arthur Peacocke [18] and I [19] have both sought to explore a little of what might be the value of such speculative, but motivated, ideas for attempts at thinking about divine providential action.

The theological discussion is balanced between a desire, on the one hand, to attain a degree of intelligibility about what might be involved in God's action in the physical world and, on the other hand, to preserve the distinctive character of deity, resisting too great a degree of assimilation of the divine to the creaturely.

One way of meeting the second need, and one which is common to all Christian thinking about God's action, is the recognition of the timeless and transcendent role of the Creator in holding the creation in being, moment by moment of its existence. In Hebrew terms, this is described by the uniquely divine word, *bara;* in theological terms, it corresponds to the concept of general providence. It makes God party to each event to the extent of the exercise of the divine permissive will in allowing that event to happen, but it does not imply that God actively desires that this should be so. Such sustaining activity has no conceivable human analogue and so it is a clear mark of divine uniqueness. Our principal

18. Peacocke, *Theology,* chs. 3 and 9.
19. J. C. Polkinghorne, *Science and Providence* (SPCK, 1989), ch. 2; *Reason and Reality,* (SPCK, 1991), ch. 3 and ref. 11.

concern, however, is with God's immanent actions within un-folding creaturely history and the deliberate results that stem from that. Here the appropriate Hebrew word might appear to be *'asah*, the ordinary word for bringing things about. The appropriate theological concept is special providence, God's particular acts on particular occasions and in particular cir-cumstances. These are the actions to which the concept of active information might have some bearing through the sup-position of the divine exercise of top-down causality. Here, also, the possibility—and some would say the danger—of in-appropriate human analogy has to be reckoned with.

Peacocke and I approach this problem in different ways. He believes that one way of achieving a satisfactory distance between a universal Creator and localised creatures is to treat God as relating to the world-as-a-whole, so that God is a global Agent, in contrast to the local actions of creatures. While God undoubtedly does relate to the whole of cre-ation, yet God surely relates to individual creatures also. It is not clear how the demands of the particularity of personal providence can convincingly be met by some unexplained trickle-down from cosmic interaction. My strategy has been to locate the Creator/creature distinction in the contrast be-tween God's acting through *pure* information input, and crea-turely acts which involve a mixture of energetic and infor-mational causalities, corresponding to the embodied status of creatures. This idea could be the prosaic translation of the-ology's poetic insight that God's action is the working of pure Spirit. I believe that such a distinction is tenable because, while passive information storage of the kind discussed by commu-nications theory does exact an irreducible energy tariff for the recording of bits of information, the same is not true for active information. Thus the concept of its pure form, unmixed with energetic causality, is a coherent one.[20]

Whatever their merits, the aim of these two strategies, Peacocke's and mine, is clear enough. It is to maintain a metaphysical distinction between God's providential agency and the intentional agency of creatures. The purpose is to absolve the proposal from the charge that it has reduced God to the role of being merely a cause among other competing causalities. The Creator, it is supposed, is more fittingly to be thought of as the director of the great cosmic improvisatory play, rather than as an invisible actor on the stage of the universe. It is not possible, however, to remove all unease about how successful either strategy actually is in this regard. The scientist-theologian is in a catch-22 situation. The more explicit the talk becomes about the causal joint by which God acts in the world, the more danger there is that providence becomes just one form of causality among others. Yet, without some such attempt at explication, the idea of providence remains too mysterious for any discussion beyond fideistic assertion.

I have recently come to reconsider whether the fundamental theological objection one is trying to meet is as forceful as I had originally supposed. What has caused this revaluation is taking the kenotic nature of God's creative act as seriously as possible. Of course, nothing could reduce talk about the Creator to terms that could bear some valid analogy to creaturely discourse, except that divine condescension had allowed this to be so. The central Christian kenotic paradox

---

20. The argument is defended partly by reference to the somewhat arcane example provided by David Bohm's causal reinterpretation of quantum theory.

of the incarnation centres on just such an act of divine self-limitation, so that God's nature is manifested in the plainest, and most accessible, creaturely terms through the Word's assumption of humanity and consequent participation in human life and human death in Jesus Christ. As the Fathers liked to say, the Ancient of Days lay as a baby in a manger. The invisible God took our flesh and became a *visible* actor on the stage of the universe. If we believe that Jesus is God incarnate then, there in first-century Palestine, God submitted in the most drastic way to being a cause among causes. Of course, that was not all that God was doing during that period. Christian theology has never simply equated God with Jesus, nor supposed that the historic episode of the incarnation implied that there was, during its period, an attentuation of the divine governance of the universe. The incarnation does, however, suggest what character that governance might at all times be expected to take. It seems that God is willing to share with creatures, to be vulnerable to creatures, to an extent not anticipated by classical theology's picture of the God who, through primary causality, is always in total control.

This thought is the inspiration for the kenotic view of creation with which our discussion began, the concept that, in allowing the other to be, God allows creatures their part in bringing about the future. There must be an intertwining of providential and creaturely causality. Such an act of divine condescension would seem to correspond precisely to God's loving choice to be, in the unfolding history of creation, an immanent cause among causes.

Twentieth-century exploration of the implication of the kenotic act of creation has progressed in successive stages. The first point to be grasped was the divine self-limitation of omnipotence. Acts of the creaturely other (whether the deed of a murderer or the incidence of a cancer) are allowed to happen, although they are not in accord with God's benevolent will. Secondly came a recognition that creation might also imply a kenosis of omniscience in that an evolving world of true becoming is one in which even the Creator does not yet know the future, for the future is not yet there to be known.[21] I am now suggesting further that divine self-emptying extends to a kenosis of the status of agency, so that special providence is exercised as a cause among causes, active within the cloudy unpredictabilities of created process. The picture of the invulnerable, all-powerful God of classical theology has given way to the picture of the God who interacts within creaturely history but does not overrule the acts of creatures.

Divine uniqueness is still maintained in a number of ways. One is God's role in the transcendent sustaining of the world in being, to which reference has already been made. Another will be in relation to miraculous action.[22] The latter is not to be understood as God's arbitrary irruption, in a quasi-magical way, into the otherwise smooth history of creation. That would involve the theological nonsense of the God of miracles acting against the same God whose faithful will is the ground of the reliable process of the universe. Rather, miracle is the revealing by the Creator of the profound potentialities that the divine will has for creation, beyond those so far discerned in the workings of the world. Divine consistency requires that there must be a deep coherence between the already known and the now being revealed. Miracle becomes

21. See, for example, Polkinghorne, *Scientists*, 41; R. Swinburne, *The Coherence of Theism*, (Oxford University Press, 1977), ch. 10.
22. Polkinghorne, *Providence*, ch. 4.

credible when these two are seen to constitute a fundamental unity. The central and essential Christian miracle of the resurrection of Jesus has just this character. It is not a hasty divine intervention on Easter Day to put right what had got badly out of hand on Good Friday, but it is the seminal event from which God's new creation has begun to grow, not as the abolition of the old creation but by way of its redemptive fulfilment.[23] (The Lord's risen body is not the replacement of his dead body, nor its resuscitation, but its glorification—hence the empty tomb.)

This leads us to another important aspect of divine uniqueness. God's purposes will eventually be fulfilled. The precariousness involved in the Creator's sharing of causality with creatures may imply that this fulfilment will be attained along contingent paths, as God responds to the free actions of others, but the God who is the ground of a true and everlasting hope will work ceaselessly to bring salvation to creation. The deep theological problems of grace and free will, and of eschatology, are not to be disposed of in the closing paragraph of a chapter on divine action, but our need to wrestle, as best we can, with the problems of God's agency arises from our religious conviction that God is no deistic spectator of the history of the universe, nor merely the sustainer of its process, but that ultimately God will be this universe's Saviour.

If the argument of this chapter contains some truth, it illustrates a necessary degree of interplay between a bottom-up approach to divine agency (arising from scientifically motivated conjecture about the causal joint by which it might be

23. See J. C. Polkinghorne, *Science and Christian Belief/The Faith of a Physicist* (SPCK/Princeton University Press, 1994), chs. 6 and 9.

exercised) and top-down theological constraint (arising from a controlling belief concerning the nature of divine love). All valid theological discourse must make some use of both approaches. It is in striking a balance between them that the best hope of achieving insight is likely to be found.

CHAPTER SEVEN

Natural Science, Temporality
and Divine Action

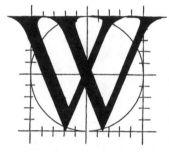

E have already noted that twentieth-century science has discovered that the universe itself has had a history—that the cosmos was very different in the past from the way it is today and that it will be different again in the future. Relativity theory has taught us that space is relational and not absolute, and that the passage of time and judgements of simultaneity are both observer-dependent assessments. We have seen that the Newtonian picture of the ceaseless rearrangements of the components of an essentially unchanging world, taking place within the fixed container of absolute space and during the steady flow of absolute time, is no longer on the scientific agenda. Instead, the universe is perceived as being relational and endowed with becoming. Yet some absolutes remain, such as the speed of light acting as the limit on the rapidity of information transfer. In relativity theory (in the scientific sense) not all dissolves into a relativistic haze (in the popular sense).

These scientific discoveries exercise some influence which flows over into metaphysics and on into theology. The connections involved are not those of strict entailment, for each discipline has its own due autonomy. Physics constrains metaphysics but it does not determine it. Yet there are certain clusters of consonant ideas that naturally associate with each other. The progression in forming such a cluster is first to abstract from science a metascientific view of aspects of physical process, then to incorporate this view within an appropriately extended metaphysical scheme, and finally to correlate with the latter a consonant theological understanding. At each stage of the construction of such a chain there is scope for argument and dissent, but certain associations of ideas emerge that seem persuasively natural and which then exert considerable influence on contemporary thinking. The purpose of this chapter is to illustrate this process by considering metascientific and metaphysical ideas about temporality and to discuss their bearing on theological concepts of God's relation to time and on understandings of divine action. In regard to this latter subject, it is God's particular action within the process of creation (special providence) which will be the focus of our attention, rather than simply the divine sustaining of the world in its orderly being (general providence).

The fact that there is an unavoidable degree of ambiguity in the results of such an exercise is illustrated at the start by the fact that one can identify four different metascientific accounts of the nature of time, each claiming to derive from contemporary physics. I shall describe them in turn, together with the metaphysical views and theological stances that seem to associate most naturally with them.

1. The passage of time is a trick of human psychological perspective.

The claim is made that the most obvious aspect of the human experience of time, the ever-moving present in which events that were future and potential are momentarily realised and become actual before receding into the fixed record of past history, is no more than the way in which we are constrained to perceive a reality which, in its fundamental nature, is actually atemporal, with all events equally real and existent, whether they are classified by us as being 'past, present or future'.

(a) *Metascience.* Those who hold this highly counterintuitive position often assert that it is a consequence of the special theory of relativity. For example, Russell Stannard writes that 'According to relativity theory, physical reality simply is'.[1] In his view, we are presented with the package deal of the space-time continuum. This seems to have been Einstein's opinion also, for on the death of his friend Michele Besso he wrote to his widow that 'Michele has left this strange world just before me. This is of no importance. For us convinced physicists the distinction between past, present and future is an illusion, though a persistent one'.[2]

Of course, the argument is not so crude as to say that the equations of relativistic physics can be written neatly and comprehensively in four-dimensional form, and why then should

---

1. R. Stannard, *Grounds for Reasonable Belief* (Scottish Academic Press, 1989), 98.
2. Quoted in I. Prigogine and I. Stengers, *Order out of Chaos* (Heinemann, 1984), 294.

one treat the dimension of time differently from the three dimensions of space? History cannot be equated with geography, or the possibility of time travel assimilated to that of motion in space, in so simple-minded a way. Instead, the argument is made in a different way and it unavoidably involves a modest degree of technical discussion.

Centred on any 'event' (spacetime point) there is the forward lightcone of future events that can be causally affected by that event, and the backward lightcone of past events that are capable of having influenced the event under consideration. These two domains are quite distinct and they are also invariant, that is to say they are the same whichever observational frame of reference is used to define them. All observers agree about them. In between, however, is a large domain of points that are spacelike in relation to the original event. This means that they can transmit no physical influence to it. This spacelike domain is four-dimensional and different observers take different three-dimensional slices through it as they define their different loci of simultaneity. (In a Newtonian world there would be a unique three-dimensional domain of simultaneity on which all observers would agree.) It is then claimed that all points in this four-dimensional spacelike domain are of equal status and so they all should be treated as equally real and existent. Shifting the location of the originating event then leads to a similar conclusion for the whole of spacetime.

I believe this argument to be fallacious. Each observer's locus of simultaneity is a *retrospective* reconstruction. No observer has knowledge of a distant event until it is unequivocally 'past', that is to say it lies in that observer's backward lightcone. There is, therefore, no special privilege attaching to these distant events, prior to their actual occurrence, of a kind that would grant them atemporal existence. The argument cannot establish the reality of the future.

Another way of establishing the same point would be to say that it is perfectly consistent with special relativity (which is here acting as a kinematical specification of the geometry of spacetime) to suppose that there is a particular frame of reference (equivalently, a definition of a preferred time axis) which expresses the actual moving present moment (and presumably coincides with our psychological perception of that present moment) *provided* that this frame does not have a special identifiable role in relation to the dynamical theories of physics. In other words, the 'present moment frame' would have to be 'hidden' as far as fundamental physics was concerned, but it could well be discernible as far as other and wider experience was concerned (human psychological perception, for instance), or as metaphysical theory might require. There is only real cause for uneasiness about this solution if one takes a physical reductionist position and insists on identifying science (more accurately, metascience) with a totally adequate metaphysical account of reality. In that case, the present moment frame would be suspect, but nothing compels this limited view.

Much the same kind of response can be made to another argument, sometimes explicitly made but more often left implicit, that because the equations of physics express in no obvious way the existence of a present moment (one might say, there is no special status for $t = 0$), such an existence is to be denied, contrary to common sense experience. 'If this is the case, so much the worse for physics', I would reply. Its inability to express the present moment is better understood as indicating the inadequacy of a reductive physicalism rather than as abolishing the idea of a moving present.

The limitations of a purely physics-based approach are further exemplified by the latter's inability to give a clear and universally accepted answer to the question of the origin of time's arrow. So far we have been discussing what the philosopher John McTaggart would have called the A-series: past-present-future. Time's arrow is a way of referring to the untensed B-series: earlier-later. With one exception (which was important at the epoch of the very early universe but which is entirely negligible today), the fundamental laws of physics are all time-reversal invariant, that is to say they make no intrinsic distinction between past and future. The direction of the arrow of time is undefined by them. Physicists have to build into the solutions of their equations this direction in which causal influences are found to propagate (technically, by selecting retarded potentials and discarding advanced potentials). It is commonly believed that time's arrow is an emergent effect of increasing complexity, with appeal being made to the second law of thermodynamics, so as to use the direction of the increasing entropy of isolated systems as the determination of the orientation of time. From this point of view, irreversibility appears to be a secondary, rather than a fundamental, property of natural process. However, the matter is still not well understood.

Since measurement is the irreversible registration of an observation, there may well be a connection here with the well-known measurement problem in quantum theory.[3] This

---

3. See, for example, J. C. Polkinghorne, *The Quantum World* (Penguin, 1990), ch. 6.

latter process implies a direction of time's arrow, since the variety of possible outcomes that might result from measuring a property of a quantum system are only resolved into a definite value found on a particular occasion *after* the act of measurement has taken place.

(b) *Metaphysics.* The foregoing metascientific view has been criticised both because it is not strictly entailed by physics, and also because of its inability to accommodate broader aspects of the human encounter with reality. If, however, these counter-arguments are overruled, or held to be of little force, then the metaphysical picture that results is clearly that of the block universe:[4] the unified totality of all spacetime events in their undifferentiated atemporal reality. Within that totality there is a B-series ordering, discriminating what precedes from what follows, but no temporal A-series ordering induced by the moving boundary between past and future.

Proponents of this view usually deny that the coexistence of the 'future' with the 'past' implies in any way a rigid determinism. Spacetime events simply are, and the question of what causal relationships there might be between them is held to be a separate issue altogether. Nevertheless, a suspicion continues to lurk in some minds that, at the very least, determinism is naturally compatible with a block universe.

(c) *Theology.* The theological view that seems consonant with a block universe is the idea of classical theology, stemming from Augustine and Boethius, that God knows the whole history of creation timelessly and 'at once' (*totum simul*). All

---

4. For a discussion of some of the issues, see C. J. Isham and J. C. Polkinghorne, 'The Debate over the Block Universe' in R. J. Russell, N. Murphy and C. J. Isham (eds.), *Quantum Cosmology and the Laws of Nature* (Vatican Observatory, 1993), 134–144.

'presents' are simultaneously known by God. In a block universe this must surely be so for, if the reality of all events is fundamentally atemporal and God knows everything as it actually is, then that divine knowledge must itself be atemporal. Conversely, if God does know everything at once, then this seems to imply a theological endorsement of the block universe and for the same reason, namely that divine knowledge is totally truthful knowledge. (Defenders of classical theism might wish to claim that if creation were temporal, God could have true knowledge of that temporality, even if it were acquired atemporally, but it does not seem clear that this is so. At issue is the question of how faithfully divine ways of knowing reflect the nature of the reality that is known.)

If God's untensed knowledge of created reality is as totally different from tensed human knowledge, as is being claimed, this might well seem to call into question the validity of any discussion of divine agency that attempted to base itself on *analogia entis* (analogy of being). In fact, as we have seen, the tradition of classical theology had recourse to the idea of God's primary agency at work in and through the secondary agencies of creatures in a way that is open neither to explication nor to exhibition. Thomas Aquinas is the patron saint of this proposition and its modern defenders have included the Anglican theologian Austin Farrer.[5] The ineffability of this claim has given rise both to the questionings of its critics and the support of its adherents.

As with the metaphysics of the block universe itself, so in relation to divine atemporal knowledge and primary causality, there has arisen the question of whether this view might not

---

5. Austin Farrer, *Faith and Speculation* (A&C Black, 1967).

incline too much towards determinism and thus carry the risk of abolishing creaturely freedom. Aquinas denied that this is so, for God does not 'foreknow' the result of a free act. Instead, in the divine simultaneous apprehension of all presents, God knows such acts as and when they happen, which no more compromises creaturely freedom than does the temporally simultaneously gained knowledge of the same act that can be acquired by another creaturely observer. Nevertheless, again some suspicions linger, not least in relation to how divine primary causality might actually relate to the secondary causality of free human actions.

At the level of the scientific observation of physical process, primary causality would seem to be indistinguishable from a scientistic naturalism. It would appear that the causal net of physical process could be drawn as tight as one liked, even to the point of a strict determinism, without theologically prejudicing the proposal. We have seen (chapter 6) that this feature is both one of its great merits in the eyes of its proposers (invulnerability to scientific discovery, whatever form that might prove to take) and also one of its great defects in the eyes of its opponents (God's presence and agency ought to make a difference to what happens). It seems strange that naturalism and primary causality can be so identical in their physics and so radically different in their metaphysics.

2. *Time is a secondary construction.*

This radical view sees temporal sequences as emerging properties in certain physical situations, but it denies to time a fundamental place in the the description of the natural world.

(a) *Metascience.* The origin of such an opinion lies in certain continuing efforts to construct a quantum theory of gravity. We have already noted (chapter 1) that quantum theory and general relativity, the two great physical theories discovered in the twentieth century, are currently imperfectly reconciled with each other. Their eventual mutual integration is obviously necessary, not only for the consistency of physics but also for the task of understanding the very early universe. General relativity is fundamental to all cosmological theorising and before the Planck time (10^{-43} seconds) the universe was small enough for quantum effects to be of great cosmic significance. Although such an infinitesimal cosmic epoch might seem extremely remote, processes occurring then are believed to have had lasting consequences for properties such as the distribution of matter in the universe.

Quantum gravity is currently an extremely uncertain and speculative discipline but one way in which attempts are being made to resolve some of its problems accords a primary role to space and a secondary role to time.[6] The rules of quantum mechanics are applied to the immense variety of spatial geometries that might be conceived to exist, and probability amplitudes (the basic quantum mechanical calculational entity) evaluated for transitions between them. In certain appropriate circumstances, a 'classical' type of trajectory can form in which a sequence of spatial geometries 'stack up' to form a succession that is susceptible to a temporal interpretation. In this particular case (which has held in our universe from about the Planck time onwards), time emerges as a contingent feature of events.

All that may seem perplexing enough. The matter is further complicated by the way in which quantum theory is being

6. See C. J. Isham, 'Quantum Theories of the Creation of the Universe' in Russell et al. (eds.), *Quantum Cosmology*, 49–89.

applied to the problem. One of the unsolved interpretative difficulties, to which we referred earlier, is the measurement problem. How does it come about that the fitful quantum world yields a definite answer on each actual occasion of its experimental interrogation, when the theory itself only assigns probabilities for a range of possible outcomes? Various proposals have been made, none completely satisfactory, of which the most generally popular has been some variation on the Copenhagen interpretation: it is due to the intervention of large 'classical' measuring apparatus. If, however, one is trying to apply quantum mechanics to the whole universe, this particular option is not available; there is nothing left over to play the role of the measuring apparatus! Quantum cosmologists have, therefore, favoured an interpretation which has not so widely recommended itself to other physicists. This is the so-called 'many-worlds' interpretation, proposed by Hugh Everett III. It is suggested that every possible outcome of an observation is in fact realised and our belief to the contrary is due to a division of the world at each such act of measurement into a series of parallel worlds in each of which only one outcome is perceived by the relevant observer to have happened. (Everett himself preferred to express this idea in terms of the 'cloning' of parallel observers.)

Clearly this is a proposal of immense prodigality in relation to the scope of physical reality. Its employment has the consequence, seldom emphasised clearly by quantum cosmologists, that in the circumstances in which a time sequence is derivable at all, there will not be just one such sequence but a vast variety of differing parallel cosmic histories.

These heady speculations are rightly called metascience

because they go far beyond what can claim the sober status of widely agreed physical understanding. Their durability as scientific ideas is open to question.

(b) *Metaphysics.* The ideas of quantum cosmology are too novel, and currently too uncertain, to have fed into any developed metaphysical account. The general picture is of a reality that at one level is fundamentally characterised by quantum mechanical disorder, but in which patches of temporal ordering emerge. Reality is multi-valued in terms of the incompatible but parallel histories that are realised within it. Yet, in another sense, the overall picture is orderly to the point of being deterministic. The basic equation that in many-worlds quantum theory plays the part one might call equivalent to 'the Schrödinger equation of the universe' (actually it is the Wheeler-DeWitt equation, which differs from the Schrödinger equation in not including a time derivative because of the secondary character of time in this formulation) is formally a perfectly deterministic linear equation in a vast array of variables. Time is secondary and emergent at one level because fundamentally the whole quantum universe, as this speculative theory understands it, simply 'is' in its variegated totality.

(c) *Theology.* At either level of interpretation (parallel worlds or overall totality), this view abolishes any notion of a true history capable of accommodating or expressing God's economy of interacting relationship with creation. Overall, there is no time but only fuzzy quantum being. In those sub-systems where 'time' emerges, there is a great variety of alternative and equally valid temporal unfoldings (a world in which Judas betrays Christ and one in which he does not?). At best, one might say that the universe is God's multi-screen experimental theatre, with every conceivable scenario being enacted. Such an account not only subverts the significance of human biography and responsibility (true moral beings could not exist in a realm of multiple happenings) but it would also be fatal to an historically based religion like Christianity.

It is interesting to consider briefly Frank Tipler's so-called 'physical theology',[7] for it operates with a many-worlds quantum cosmology. Tipler's treatment is strongly physical-ist and reductionist. Human beings are treated as finite state machines (computers) and life is equated to the processing of information. A final state boundary condition is imposed on 'the wavefunction of the universe' that requires that in the dying final fractions of a second of a collapsing cosmos, all parts of it are in causal contact with each other. This is held to facilitate the coming-to-be of a cosmic computer, Omega (a 'physical god' in Tipler's phrase), whose ever-faster racing operations will permit the processing of an infinite number of bits of information in the course of the approach to the ultimate event of the universe's death. Tipler regards this conjectural achievement as fulfilling a 'physical eschatology', claiming that Omega will 'resurrect' persons by constructing emulations (computer copies) of the fleshly computers that they once were when biologically alive.

It is all extremely fantastic and the proposal has made little impression on theologians with a scientific background.[8]

---

7. F. J. Tipler, *The Physics of Immortality* (Macmillan, 1994).

8. I. G. Barbour, *Religion in an Age of Science* (SCM Press, 1990), 151; A. R. Peacocke, *Theology for a Scientific Age* (SCM Press, enlarged edition 1993), 345; J. C. Polkinghorne, *Science and Christian Belief/The Faith of a Physicist* (SPCK/Princeton University Press, 1994), 165–166.

For our present purpose we can regard the baroque conjectures of physical eschatology as giving a measure of the actual theological vacuity of this point of view of the nature of time.

3. The evolution of time is a closed process.

Time is treated as a measure of the stage of development of a physical process that is causally closed upon itself. The laws of physics control the state of the world and determine fully how one such state gives rise to its temporal successor. This is the picture which many people, including it seems some theologians, believe is the deliverance of modern science: the clockwork universe. Others believe that the uncertainties of quantum mechanics have negated this account as far as subatomic processes are concerned, but they are unsure what implications this carries for the macroscopic world in which all human action and experience seems to be located.

(a) *Metascience.* The distinction between science and metascience is made abundantly clear by the existence of rival interpretations of the fundamental character of quantum theory. Heisenberg's uncertainty principle is a statement about limitations on the precision attainable in measurements made on quantum systems. In other words, originally it was an epistemological result, referring to what we can know. The great majority of physicists have followed Heisenberg and Bohr in interpreting it ontologically, that is to say as expressing an actual degree of indeterminacy in the behaviour of quantum entities. This interpretation is the basis of the widespread belief that the quantum world displays a degree of causal openness towards the future and that its probabilistic nature is the expression of a rift in a tight causal nexus. However, there is no forced move from epistemology to ontology and a minority of physicists have wanted to hold on to a deterministic account of quantum phenomena, with probabilism then arising from our ignorance of all the causal determinants actually at work. Causes of this covert kind are given the generic name 'hidden variables'. David Bohm constructed just such an account of quantum theory,[9] which is identical to conventional quantum mechanics in its experimental consequences but totally contrasting in its picture of the nature of physical process. The choice between Bohr and Bohm is metascientific. It is based on such criteria as judgements of naturalness and lack of contrivance, and on metaphysical preferences for determinism or open process, but not on tests of empirical adequacy. It is, therefore, perfectly possible in the twenty-first century to hold an account of the physical world that is as unproblematically objective and deterministic as was the eighteenth-century mechanics of Newton and Laplace.

Contrary to the claim sometimes made by theologians,[10] this statement is not modified by the nineteenth-century discovery, stemming from the insights of Faraday and Maxwell, of the existence of fields. A classical field is a perfectly mechanical system, differing in its nature from the mechanics of particles only by the fact that it involves an infinite number of degrees of freedom (distinct ways in which it can change) rather than a finite number. The mathematical consequence of this is that field theory is expressed in terms of partial differential equations rather than ordinary differential equations, but both kinds of equation are equally deterministic. One may also

9. D. Bohm and B. Hiley, *The Undivided Universe* (Routledge, 1993).
10. See chapter 8.

note that classical fields are *local* entities, that is to say independent changes can be made at spatially separated points because there is no integrated constraint imposed on the structure of the whole.

(b) *Metaphysics*. Because perfect knowledge of the present implies for a deterministic system perfect prediction of the future and perfect retrodiction of the past (Laplace's celebrated calculating demon with universal knowledge), it is possible to assimilate the apparently temporal metaphysics of this option to the atemporal picture of option 1. Traditionally, however, this has not been the strategy followed and a deterministic universe has usually been considered temporally, despite, as we noted earlier, there being no intrinsic way of representing the present moment in its equations. The mathematically minded could picture the moving present as being the unfolding surface of solutions as the deterministic equations are integrated from the starting point of their initial conditions. A computer would generate a time-dependent solution in just this successive fashion, so that one could think of the history of a universe of this type as being the analogue integration of the equations of the fundamental theory.

(c) *Theology*. Because of the feasibility of assimilating option 3 to option 1, it would be possible to associate with a closed universe the theological picture of divine primary causality acting in and under its tight secondary determinism. One must emphasise again, however, that those classical theologians who defend the notion of primary causality do so whilst repudiating strict physical determinism and claiming the compatibility of divine atemporal knowledge with temporal human choice and responsibility.

Much the most common theological response to a closed universe has been that of deism. In a clockwork world the Creator has nothing much to do except be the Cosmic Clockmaker who set it all up and now simply lets it tick away. One sees this view developing in the eighteenth century among the post-Newtonian generations. Sir Isaac himself certainly did not think this way, for he saw a causal role for spirits (for example, producing every fifty thousand years or so angelic corrections to the motion of the solar system which otherwise, he feared, might have wobbled apart), and he made his celebrated but mysterious assertion that space was the '*sensorium* of God'. His successors tended to think otherwise. To them, the God of deism then became too much of an absentee landlord to carry much conviction and the transition to accept atheism came relatively easily.

The contemporary atemporal deism of Maurice Wiles,[11] which simply assigns to the deity the single great act of holding the world in being, is in the same tradition. One feels that Wiles does not wish to risk a divine interruption into what he believes to be the self-contained process of the universe. An unnecessary deference to a particular and contentious meta-scientific account has been allowed to induce impotence in theological thinking about special providential divine action.
4. The evolution of time is an open process.

While acknowledging the role of a physical causality that is expressed through the interchange of energy between constituent parts, this option suggests that these effects do not suffice to determine completely the temporal development of

11. M. F. Wiles, *God's Action in the World* (SCM Press, 1986).

the world. There is held to be scope for the action of additional causal principles that serve to bring about the future. What character these principle might have is discussed below.

(a) *Metascience.* Contemporary understanding of physical process detects within it a considerable degree of intrinsic unpredictability, both within quantum theory and within chaos theory.[12] There is a large and inescapable epistemological deficit in our knowledge of the behaviour of physical process. The critical metascientific question is what ontological significance, if any, is to assigned to this fact.

I have argued [13] that the realist philosophy that is so natural a stance for a scientist to take encourages us to align epistemology and ontology as closely as possible with each other. In other words, intrinsic unpredictability is to be treated as the signal of an underlying ontological openness. In fact, as we have already seen, this is indeed the policy embraced by most physicists in relation to quantum theory.

In the case of chaos theory, the majority approach has been different. The most popular metascientific conclusion has been to take absolutely seriously the deterministic equations from which classical chaos derives and to draw the lesson that apparently complex and random behaviour can have a simple and deterministic underlying origin. This is, of course, a perfectly permissible metascientific choice to make and it has doubtless been encouraged by the fact that the underlying structure in this case would be the time-honoured Newtonian equations of motion. It is not, however, the only pos-

12. J. Gleick, *Chaos* (Heinemann, 1988).
13. J. C.Polkinghorne, *Reason and Reality* (SPCK, 1991), ch. 3. See also chapter 6 in this book.

sible metascientific strategy. I have proposed the alternative of a realist reading in which the classical unpredictabilities are taken to be signals of openness.[14] Newton's equations are then to be treated as downward emergent *approximations* to a more subtle and supple physical reality, approximations that are valid in those special circumstances in which parts can adequately be isolated from the whole in which they participate. As we have seen in chapter 6, there then emerges the concept of a new kind of causality, complementing the energetic bottom-up causal exchanges between parts described by conventional physics, and having the character of top-down, holistic pattern formation. I have called this metascientific picture 'contextualism' (for the behaviour of constituents varies with the context they are set in), and the corresponding causal principles 'active information'.

It would be possible to consider a hybrid scheme in which the widely assumed openness of quantum events had its consequences amplified and made apparent in the macroscopic world through the sensitivity of chaotic systems to small fluctuations occurring at the subatomic level. There are, however, technical problems that make this proposal problematic. One is our inability to solve the measurement problem in quantum theory. With this question unresolved, we are ignorant of precisely how the microscopic and macroscopic levels relate to each other. Another difficulty has been the inability to identify clearly what the quantum mechanical equivalent of chaos is. The hybrid scheme may well prove to be part of the meta-

---

14. J. C. Polkinghorne, *Belief in God in an Age of Science* (Yale University Press, 1998), ch. 3. See also, I. Prigogine, *The End of Certainty* (Free Press, 1997).

scientific picture being developed, but it would be unwise to rely on it alone.

(b) *Metaphysics*. This particular approach extends our conception of the range of causal principles that may be thought to be at work in determining the open future. Among possible consequences of active information might be:

(i) Holistic laws of nature which facilitate the coming-to-be of certain kinds of complexity. Stuart Kauffman has made a proposal of this kind in relation to biological evolution.[15]

(ii) There might here be a glimmer (no more) of how one might begin to conceive of the relationship between mind (intention—like pattern forming) and brain (physical activity—like energetic exchange).

(iii) Theology is offered the possibility of beginning to understand its discourse of God's special providential action, often expressed in terms of the Spirit's guiding creation, in terms of a divine interaction within the world through active information.

All three kinds of causal activity would be at work within the non-localisable, unpredictable cloudiness of chaotic systems. While these effects would genuinely share in determining the future, they would not be disentangleable from each other or unambiguously identifiable. One could not itemise physical process, saying 'Nature did this, human agency did that, God did the other'.

15. S. A. Kauffman, *The Origins of Order* (Oxford University Press, 1993).

A reality within which such a variety of causal principles would be at work is clearly one in which temporal process is to be taken absolutely seriously. This option presents a metaphysics of dynamical becoming, in contrast to one of static being. The future is not up there waiting for us to arrive; we play our part in bringing it about, for it is contingent upon our executed intentions as well as on the operation of other causalities and agencies.

(c) *Theology*. The option under discussion has the attraction of allowing scope for the operation of divine special providence in the history of the universe. Because of the hidden character of active information, God's action will not be demonstrable, though it may be discernible by the discriminating eye of faith. The balance between divine agency and other forms of causality is left open in this proposal which, therefore, has to continue the long theological discussion of the relationship between grace and free will, considered now in a cosmic setting. A critical theological question is whether the cost of the idea would be unacceptable because it seemed to reduce the Creator to the role of an unseen cause among creaturely causes, an issue already discussed in chapter 6.

The strongly temporal character of the metaphysics proposed seems to imply that God, knowing the universe as it actually is, would know it temporally. The future would be brought into being as time evolves and it would appear that God, knowing all that can be known, would nevertheless not yet know the unformed future. God's act of creation would not only have involved a divine kenosis of omnipotence, resulting from allowing the creaturely other truly to be itself, but also a divine kenosis of omniscience, arising from allowing the future to be truly open.

Thus the theological picture consonant with this option is one that sees in the divine nature a temporal pole of engagement with creation as well as, of course, an eternal pole corresponding to the steadfastly unchanging benevolent nature of God. There would be divine knowledge of creation, always complete in terms of realised history but not embracing a future that is open and not yet actualised. These ideas have been supported by a number of people writing on the interface between science and theology.[16]

PROCESS THOUGHT

Such a dipolar view of God, and of divine current omniscience, has also been a characteristic of process thinking.[17] It may seem surprising that a process option was not included in the foregoing discussion. The reason for its omission lies at the metascientific level in the chain of argument. The punctuated discrete events ('actual occasions'), which form the basis of the picture of the nature of physical process presented in the thought of A. N. Whitehead and his followers, are difficult to reconcile with our scientific knowledge. Conventional quantum theory certainly has its discrete moments of discontinuous change ('the collapse of the wavepacket'), but they are only associated with a particular kind of event, namely measurements. In between such macroscopic interventions, a quantum system evolves in a perfectly smooth and continuous way, according to the rule of the Schrödinger equation. Therefore, I do not detect a point of anchorage for process metaphysics

16. See J. C. Polkinghorne, *Scientists as Theologians* (SPCK, 1996), 41
17. In the context of science and theology, see Barbour, *Religion*, ch. 8.

in what we know about physics. Thus the generalising chain of consonant concepts, which we discussed in connection with the four selected options, appears broken at its first link in the case of process thought. The final link would also be suspect, since process theologians' view of God's action is based solely on the power of divine persuasion, with the ultimate initiative lying with the concrescing event itself. This, in my opinion, presents too weak an account to be adequate to accommodate the Christian experience of prayer or the Christian intuition of God's providence at work in history.

One might claim that the ontological interpretation of chaos theory offers an opportunity to express some of the more theologically congenial aspects of process thinking (such as the openness of creation to the future) in a way that is scientifically more persuasive. A similar comment might also be made about some of the ideas of Teilhard de Chardin.[18] His concept of 'radial energy' corresponds to nothing that is scientifically recognisable in conventional energetic terms, but it could be reinterpreted as a metaphor for the effect of active information.

18. P. Teilhard de Chardin, *The Phenomenon of Man*, (Collins, 1959).

Part III

SIGNIFICANT THINKERS

CHAPTER EIGHT

Contemporaries

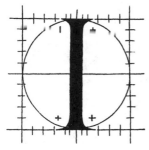

N my book *Scientists as Theologians*,[1] I surveyed the thinking of three scientist-theologians, Ian Barbour, Arthur Peacocke and myself. For each of us, our intellectual formation had lain in science and it was only later in life that we turned to theology. In the course of this comparative study of our writings on science and theology, there emerged both important common themes and also significant differences of approach and conclusion among the three of us. I acknowledged that I was leaving out of the account both theologians who pay some attention to modern science in their writings and also scientists who display an interest in a theistic view of reality but who are not adherents of any faith tradition. I now wish to remedy this deficit to some extent by considering the relevant ideas of Wolfhart Pannenberg and Thomas Torrance, both outstanding examples of the

---

1. J. C. Polkinghorne, *Scientists as Theologians* (SPCK, 1996).

first category, and of Paul Davies, an outstanding example of the second category.

8.1 WOLFHART PANNENBERG'S ENGAGEMENT WITH THE NATURAL SCIENCES

Wolfhart Pannenberg is unquestionably one of the leading theologians of the second half of the twentieth century. His thought is of particular interest to those of us whose intellectual formation lies in the natural sciences. There are many reasons why this should be so. One is Pannenberg's open approach to theology, acknowledging the possibility of its being in need of correction and allowing an appeal to evidence as the ground for motivated belief, not least in relation to the resurrection of Christ. This suggests the existence of a degree of intellectual kinship between theology and science. Another reason, of a most direct kind to catch the attention of scientists, is that Pannenberg himself expresses a serious concern with what the natural sciences have to say. Not for him the life of the theological ghetto, which some of his fellow practitioners seem to occupy, in which a special language is spoken, allowing no discourse with those tongues whose utterance lies outside that closed world. Pannenberg is a firm believer in the unity of knowledge, a conviction derived from his belief in the one true God whose creative will is the ground of all that is. Scientists are instinctive synthesisers, looking for the integrated account that a grand unified theory can confer, and so this all-embracing view is very congenial to their intellectual inclination.

Pannenberg's writings are voluminous and demanding. It is, therefore, a great benefit that there is a single volume in which some of his essays of particular relevance to science are gathered together; his thought is discussed by a variety of scientists, philosophers and theologians; and he himself responds at the end to this vigorous debate.[2] Its editor, Carol Rausch Albright, provides clear and sure-footed introductory prefaces to the successive sections into which the material is organised—a guide to the labyrinth which will be appreciated by many readers.

The foundation of Pannenberg's thinking is his belief in God as the all-determining reality. In his opinion, there is no realm of human enquiry or area of human experience from which God is excluded or which can be fully intelligible without taking into account the divine will and purpose that undergirds it. Here is the modern formulation of the scholastic concept of theology as the Queen of the Sciences, understanding 'science' in the medieval sense of *scientia*, all knowledge, and with theology's regal status deriving from its access to the deepest and most comprehensive ground of intelligibility, rather than from a presumed prescriptive right to tell the other individual sciences what to think at the level of their first-order enquiries. The critical question here is one of *scope*. Other particular sciences pursue a limited range of enquiry; theology is unlimited in the width of its considerations, for it is 'not concerned with this or that being in its particularity, or with one area of reality which can be separated from others . . . [but] with reality in general'.[3]

2. C. R. Albright and J. Haugen (eds.), *Beginning with the End* (Open Court, 1997); see also the collection of Pannenberg's essays in T. Peters (ed.), *Towards a Theology of Nature* (Westminster/John Knox, 1993).

3. W. Pannenberg, *Theology and the Philosophy of Science* (Darton, Longman and Todd, 1976), 303.

In relation to the natural sciences, this leads Pannenberg to write,

> If the God of the Bible is the creator of the universe, then it is not possible to understand fully or even appropriately the processes of nature without any reference to that God. If, on the contrary, nature can be appropriately understood without reference to the God of the Bible, then that God cannot be the creator of the universe, and consequently he cannot be truly God and be trusted as a source of moral teaching either.[4]

The last remark is clearly intended as a refutation of the Kantian programme that allocated the physical world to science and the moral sphere to religion. Some care would be needed in evaluating what such a claim about the processes of nature could actually amount to.

The manifest success of a *methodologically* atheistic natural science, often pursued with great insight by people of no religious belief, shows that it would be implausible to suggest too direct an influence of theology upon the researches of science. Moreover, such a claim of the relative independence of the natural sciences could find a degree of theological support. We have seen that an important aspect of much twentieth-century theological thinking about the doctrine of creation has been an emphasis on the kenotic character of the Creator's act.[5] A letting-be by divine love of the truly other, allowed by God to be itself, carries with it the implication of a degree of due in-

4. Albright and Haugen, *Beginning*, 38.
5. See J. Moltmann, *God in Creation* (SCM Press, 1985), ch. 4. See also chapter 6 in this volume.

dependence granted to creatures. We may understand this as being the theological source of science's ability to pursue its investigations *etsi deus non daretur*, as if God did not exist.

From the biblical material, one might also draw attention to the wisdom literature of the Old Testament. The wisdom writers take a cool look at what is happening in the world, describing it in terms of sufficient theological neutrality as to enable them to add to it borrowings from similar writings drawn from the surrounding cultures. References to YHWH, where present at all, take the form of general exhortations to remember that the fear of the Lord is the beginning of wisdom and there is no specific appeal to God's acts of deliverance and judgement within history, of the kind that forms so great a matter of concern in the rest of the Hebrew scriptures. The wisdom writers presumably held that there were things that could be understood without such an appeal.

Where theological understanding does come in to augment and complement scientific understanding is in relation to certain limit questions that arise out of scientific experience but which transcend science's own self-limited range of enquiry. They revolve around two fundamental metaquestions:

(1) Why is the universe so deeply intelligible? Putting it more bluntly, Why is science possible? Our ability to understand the physical world seems vastly to exceed anything that could plausibly be held to correspond to evolutionary necessity, or to be a happy accidental spin-off from survival requirements. Science exploits the wonderful rational transparency of the physical world, but it does not explain it. If the universe is the creation of the rational God, then it is possible to under-

stand its intelligibility as due to its being shot through with signs of the mind of its Creator, signs that are accessible to the thoughts of creatures made in the image of the Creator.

(2) Why is the universe so special? This question arises from the recognition, enshrined in the Anthropic Principle, that the laws of nature are fine-tuned to the high degree of specificity found to be necessary to make the evolution of carbon-based life a possibility. There are a variety of responses possible to the issues raised here. Theism is not the only conceivable answer, but it is one that is coherent, economic and intellectually satisfying.

Considering metaquestions of this kind takes us beyond science in the direction of the deeper and more comprehensive understanding that theism can provide. Such arguments have been the basis of a revival in natural theology.[6]

There are also further theological insights that complement understandings drawn from science but which correspond to a theology of nature rather than a natural theology. The latter frames its arguments in terms of rumours of God derived 'from below', appealing to the intelligibility and fruitfulness of the world, in contrast to the former's insights derived 'from above', appealing to the concept of the Creator to give greater understanding of the processes of that world. A prime example would be the the theological insight we have already espoused that interprets an evolutionary universe, not as being the meaningless empire of accident proclaimed by atheist biologists such as Jacques Monod and Richard

---

6. See P. Davies, *The Mind of God* (Simon and Schuster, 1992); J. C. Polkinghorne, *Science and Creation* (SPCK, 1998), chs. 1 and 2.

Dawkins,[7] but as a creation allowed by God to explore and realise the potentiality with which it has been endowed.[8]

Pannenberg's actual engagement with the natural sciences has not been in such specific terms as are involved either in the discussion of natural theology or of a theology of nature. He has certainly sought to conduct a detailed dialogue with the human sciences,[9] an interface with theology which is obviously of the highest significance for both disciplines. Indeed Pannenberg has gone so far as to say that 'The meaning of the word "God" can, since the beginning of modern times, be determined only by anthropology'.[10] Yet, in contrast, his intercourse with the physical and biological sciences has been conducted in very general terms. It has revolved around three broad topics, each characteristic also of Pannenberg's wider theological concerns.

(i) *The concept of field.* This is, perhaps, the most baffling aspect of Pannenberg's thought for the scientist to confront. His writings abound with reference to fields as expressions of divine presence and as significant entities in other ways as well. The first problem is how seriously should the language be taken? If the word 'field' is just being used in a non-specific sense to signify something involving the notion of extended relationality, then the scientist could have nothing to quarrel with except to express a regret that a word with a pre-

7. J. Monod, *Chance and Necessity* (Collins, 1972); R. Dawkins, *The Blind Watchmaker* (Longman, 1986).

8. See I. G. Barbour, *Issues in Science and Religion* (SCM Press, 1966), ch. 12; A. R. Peacocke, *Creation and the World of Science* (Oxford University Press, 1979).

9. W. Pannenberg, *Anthropology in Theological Perspective* (Westminster, 1985).

10. Pannenberg in Peters, *Theology of Nature*, 81.

cise meaning in physics was being employed in this rather vague way. However, this does not seem to be all that is going on. References to Faraday (but not many references to the enormous development of the field concept that followed in physics during the next one hundred and fifty years) seem to suggest a more focussed appeal to scientific parallels.

We are told that by 'field' Pannenberg means 'the inter-penetrating network of energetic forces which are woven into relational patterns'.[11] Note the word 'energetic', which seems to point clearly in the direction of physics. It is important to recognise that energy is not a kind of 'spiritual' concept. Einstein's famous equation, $E = mc^2$, as much asserts the materiality of energy as it does the energetic character of matter. A physical field, like Maxwell's electromagnetic field, carries energy and momentum, inertial properties which function in the same way for the field as they do for particles of matter. Pannenberg does not seem to recognise that this is so. After a long historical discussion of the word 'spirit', noting among other things the Stoic notion of *pneuma* as subtle matter, he feels that we have progressed beyond a kind of etiolated materialism for 'difficulties of this kind no longer burden the field concept of modern physics, at least if no ether is considered necessary for the expansion of waves within the field'.[12] This notion of a field's immateriality is clearly not correct. The physicist cannot be other than profoundly uneasy when Pannenberg writes 'I rather think that the modern conception of fields and energy went a long way to 'spiritualise' physics'.[13]

11. Albright and Haugen, *Beginning*, 251.
12. Pannenberg in Peters, *Theology of Nature*, 39–40.
13. Albright and Haugen, *Beginning*, 429.

If there is a hint of a move in modern physics in the direction that Pannenberg desires, it does not arise from field theory but from the discoveries of chaos theory and complexity theory.[14] The discovery of the spontaneous generation of large-scale orderly structures in complex systems, both in space and in time, has led to a recognition that notions of energetic causality need supplementing by notions of a kind of pattern-forming causality, for which some of us have coined the phrase 'active information'.[15] If there is a hint of the emergence of the 'spiritual' in modern science, this is where it is to be found and not in field theory as such. The behaviour of these complex physical systems also manifests irreversibility (the distinction between past and future, defining a direction for the arrow of time). This is a property to which Pannenberg attaches great significance, because of his emphasis on the role of a genuinely unfolding history of creation.

The same set of scientific discoveries also encourages the recognition of the need to think holistically in addition to thinking in constituent terms. Chaotic systems are so sensitive to circumstances that they can never be treated in isolation from their environment. Spontaneously generated order appears as a property of the whole. We have seen that even quantum theory is found to bear witness to the non-atomistic nature of physical reality by its discovery of the 'EPR effect'. The holistic view of the significance of wholes over parts, to which Pannenberg rightly attaches great importance, derives,

14. See, for example, J. Gleick, *Chaos* (Heinemann, 1988); S. Kauffman, *The Origins of Order* (Oxford University Press, 1993).

15. A. R. Peacocke, *Theology for a Scientific Age* (SCM Press, 1993) chs. 3 and 9; J. C. Polkinghorne, *Reason and Reality* (SPCK, 1991), ch. 3; *Belief in God in an Age of Science* (Yale University Press, 1998), ch. 3. See also chapter 6 in this volume.

as far as natural science is concerned, to a significant degree from our growing insight into the way in which complexity generates emergent novelty, and not from field theory. In fact, contrary to what Pannenberg appears to believe, a classical field is a *local* entity. It is indeed spread out over the whole of space, but its values can be varied independently at points which are spatially separated from each other. They are not tied together into an integrated whole.

Where modern field theory does express a kind of integrated synthesis is in its quantised form. Quantum field theory resolves the paradox of wave/particle duality. All fields have wavelike properties because of their spatial extension, but the addition of quantum mechanics introduces also a countable discreteness. The energetic excitations of the field then come in packets (quanta), which are given a particle interpretation. In modern physical thinking, particles and fields belong together as a single entity, the former being excitations in the latter. In a powerful concept pioneered by Richard Feynman, the interactions of fields are conveyed by the exchange of virtual particles corresponding to them.

It is not the case that fields as such have any intrinsic relationship to contingency. We have seen that the difference classically between a collection of particles and a field is simply that the former has a finite number of degrees of freedom (distinct ways in which their state of motion can change), and the latter has an infinite number of degrees of freedom. This results in particles being described by ordinary differential equations and fields by partial differential equations. Both sets of equations are equally deterministic; correctly set boundary conditions specify completely the subsequent temporal development of their solutions. Of course, quantum fields do display contingent behaviour, but that arises from their quantum mechanical, rather than their field theoretic, nature.

(ii) *Contingency.* Pannenberg places great emphasis on the contingency of creation. This is understood in two distinct senses. One affirms the total dependence of the universe upon its Creator, who freely holds it in being, moment by moment. The other relates to the reality and significance of history, which is no mere unrolling of an already written scroll but the unfolding development of a world of true becoming. Both these concepts are fundamental to Christian theology and Pannenberg's strong defence of them is very welcome. He believes that they were threatened by the development of the scientific idea of inertia, adumbrated in the late middle ages, articulated by Galileo and Newton, and expressed in modern physics by the conservation laws (of energy, momentum, angular momentum, etc.), which play so important a role in the contemporary understanding of nature. Pannenberg defines inertia as 'an innate potential of persistence for any physical entity, be it in a state of rest or in a state of motion, unless it is disturbed by some other force'.[16] He believes the notion has exercised a pernicious influence on theology. In his view, it led to the idea of the self-sustaining character of matter and so it encouraged a line of thought leading to the redundancy of the Creator. While historically this may well have been the case, it is clear that there was never a theological necessity that this should be so. Conservation laws are as contingent as any other part of the laws of nature. Physically, they arise in a deep way as consequences of the symmetry principles with which nature is endowed. Theologically, conser-

16. Albright and Haugen, *Beginning*, 41.

vation laws, and the symmetries that give rise to them, are to be understood to continue only as long as the Creator sustains them in being. This aspect of contingency is radically metaphysical in character and so it can neither be asserted nor denied simply on the basis of any form of physical theory.

The second sense of contingency, relating to the character of physical process, is also metaphysical in its nature, but in a way that is more open to influence from physics. It must be admitted that the openness of the future would be hard to defend in the rigidly deterministic universe that Laplace regarded as the inexorable consequence of taking Newtonian ideas seriously. We have seen that in that world, full knowledge of the present, together with unlimited calculating power, implied also total knowledge of a rigorously entailed past and future. Nothing really novel ever happened; history was a reiterated tautology. However, the iron grip of Laplace's calculating demon has been relaxed by the twentieth century discovery of widespread *intrinsic* unpredictabilities present in nature, both at the microscopic level of quantum events and also at the macroscopic level of the behaviour of exquisitely sensitive chaotic systems. We have noted already that the question of whether these epistemological deficiencies are to be interpreted as signs of an ontological openness is a metaphysical issue, not to be settled by the natural sciences alone. In the case of chaotic systems, we have seen that it is possible to develop an interpretation that leads to the existence of extra causal principles with the form of the 'active information', and that these might well be capable of accommodating the action of both human and divine agency.[17] Such a programme would then

17. See Polkinghorne, *Belief in God*, ch. 3.

achieve Pannenberg's desired defence of the openness of history, as theology wishes to understand it, not by appeal to field theory but to the ideas of the top-down effects of active information. There is much that is necessarily speculative here, but I believe that these ideas afford a better model than field for the presence and activity of the Spirit. The emphasis on pattern-making certainly seems consistent with Pannenberg's idea of Spirit as a 'presence of meaning'.[18]

(iii) *The future.* Perhaps the most distinctive aspect of Pannenberg's thinking has been his emphasis on the role of the future, conceived not simply as the location of the fulfilment of divine purpose at the end of history, but as the locus of a retrospective drawing power, guiding history in the direction that God wills for it: 'it is from the future that the abiding essence of things discloses itself'.[19] There is in Pannenberg's thinking a fundamental 'assumption of the priority of the future over past and present'.[20]

Oddly enough, there is a rather banal way in which science could accommodate this notion. It is well-known that the field equations of physics admit of two, mutually exclusive forms of solution. One is based on what are called retarded potentials and it describes a situation in which effects propagate from past to future; the other is based on advanced potentials and it describes a situation in which effects propagate from the future into the past. However, it is a physical fact (whose origin is not well understood) that our universe appears to be one whose processes are generated by retarded potentials only. In our world, the bell rings only after the but-

18. Pannenberg, *Anthropology*, 520.
19. Ibid., 525.
20. Albright and Haugen, *Beginning*, 428.

ton has been pressed. (It is amusing to note, however, that Fred Hoyle has made a highly speculative proposal that the Intelligence he believes brings about much of the order in our world operates from the future by influencing the outcomes of quantum events.[21])

One cannot help feeling that Pannenberg's idiosyncratic view of the divine power of the future is his way of expressing the Christian conviction of the ultimate eschatological triumph of God. Two comments can be made. One is that it is perfectly possible to combine ordinary notions of causality, provided they are open enough to accommodate a concept of God's active providential agency, with the belief that the determinate divine purposes will be fulfilled, albeit along contingent paths.[22] The often-used parable, at least as old as William James, of the divine Grandmaster winning the game of cosmic chess, whatever moves are made by the creaturely opponent, while not wholly satisfactory, carries something of the flavour of this idea.

A second comment relates to the nature of the eschatological fulfilment that can be anticipated. It will surely be characterised both by continuity with the past (it is truly historical creatures whose destined redemption is achieved) and also by discontinuity (so that there is a new creation, released from the transience and suffering of the old creation into an everlasting world made sacramental by the divine presence within it).[23] We find Paul wrestling in 1 Corinthians 15 with the problem of what such continuity/discontinuity could mean.

21. F. Hoyle, *The Intelligent Universe* (Michael Joseph, 1983), ch. 8.

22. See D. Bartholomew, *God of Chance* (SCM Press, 1984), ch. 4.

23. J. C. Polkinghorne, *Science and Christian Belief/The Faith of a Physicist* (SPCK/Princeton University Press, 1994), ch. 9; cf. *Beginning*, 438.

The transformative dimension of this hope sets limits to the validity of any eschatological extrapolation from our understanding of present process. Our best clue lies in the resurrection of Christ, so vigorously defended by Pannenberg as being an enacted event within history, though with a reach beyond history.[24] Here is located, in the midst of time, the seminal event from which the new creation will grow, as the redeemed transformation of the old creation (just as the Lord's risen body was the glorified form of his dead body—hence the empty tomb).

It is time to return to less specific issues. In view of Pannenberg's very general, and to some degree questionable, engagement with broad topics related to physics, it is somewhat surprising to read his words that 'the attempt to find some common ground with physics has occupied more of my time than engagement with any other discipline, except perhaps history'.[25] One might have hoped that greater attention would have been given to the content of modern physical theory. No doubt the need for revision, due to the unanticipated discoveries made as scientific exploration advances, does mean that the conclusions of the natural sciences have the character of 'provisional versions of objective reality',[26] but nevertheless, in a well-winnowed physical regime, the understandings gained can be expected to have lasting stability. We are not going to change our minds about the atomic constitution of matter!

On the comparatively rare occasions when Pannenberg does consider specific scientific ideas, there can be a some-

24. W. Pannenberg, *Jesus, God and Man* (SCM Press, 1968).
25. Albright and Haugen, *Beginning,* 435.
26. Ibid., 405.

what portentous character to what is said. The spontaneous emergence of large-scale order in dissipative systems, held far from equilibrium, is a striking phenomenon, but it seems a little grandiose to describe it as 'ecstatic self-transcendence', words also employed to describe an organism's ecological relationships.[27] There are also occasional errors. It is misleading to say that the Weak Anthropic Principle specifies that 'the emergence of life and intelligence in the universe cannot be considered an accidental feature'.[28] What it does say is simply that the state of the universe as we observe it must be compatible with our presence as observers within it, a virtually tautologous statement amounting merely to the recognition that if neither the cosmic age nor the cosmic circumstances were such as to have permitted our emergence, we would not be in existence to do the observing. (We see a universe about fifteen billion years old because it takes that long to evolve men and women from the original ball of energy of the big bang.)

Among the dangers in venturing into a discipline beyond one's own is that of succumbing to gullibility. No doubt scientists who make forays into theology are by no means exempt from this peril. Nor is Pannenberg in his engagement with physical science. This is most evident in the enthusiastic welcome he gave at first to the speculative ideas of Frank Tipler. Pannenberg is certainly not without his reservations,[29] but in general he takes Tipler much more seriously than, say, the scientist-theologians[30] are inclined to do. In *Beginning with the End*, Tipler presents an account of his views in relatively mea-

27. Ibid., 104–107.
28. Ibid., 437.
29. Ibid., 437–441.
30. See Polkinghorne, *Scientists*, 53.

sured terms[31] and he receives from some of his fellow contributors a quizzically respectful response. However, subsequent to the 1988 symposium on which that volume is based, Tipler published a much fuller version of his thinking in his book *The Physics of Immortality*.[32] This made clear the chilling reductionism of the proposal (human beings are regarded as information-processing finite state machines) and its fantastically speculative character, not only metaphysically but also physically (assumptions are made about the behaviour of matter in regimes less than 10^{-N} seconds away from the final singularity, where $N = 10^{10}$, whilst even those bold speculators, the quantum cosmologists discussing the very early universe, do not pretend to get much closer to a singularity than 10^{-43} seconds).

Pannenberg tells us that 'the most comprehensive issue arising from theological dialogue with the sciences is certainly that of cosmology'.[33] If that is the case, it would be best to rely on the well-founded prediction of eventual cosmic death, either through collapse or decay, than on Tipler's fantastic imaginary scenario. The final futility of present physical process poses precisely the question that eschatology has to address: Does the universe make total sense or is it, as Steven Weinberg notoriously said, ultimately 'pointless'?[34] The answer surely lies in the Christian concept of death and resurrection, rather than in the the kind of extreme evolutionary optimism proposed by Tipler (and, one must say, in a different way by Teilhard de Chardin). Of course, Pannenberg—

---

31. Albright and Haugen, *Beginning*, 156-194.
32. F. J. Tipler, *The Physics of Immortality* (Doubleday, 1994).
33. Albright and Haugen, *Beginning*, 436.
34. S. Weinberg, *The First Three Minutes* (A. Deutsch, 1977), 149.

the theologian of hope and of the resurrection—knows that this is so. Concerning the death of the universe, he says, 'new life could well be remembered in God's eternity so it could be resurrected at the end of history'[35], but he does not make enough of this fundamental insight.

The themes of this section have been quite critical of details of Pannenberg's engagement with the natural sciences. It is to be hoped that the reader will perceive beneath these themes the *cantus firmus* of an admiration for a great theologian who is not content to dwell in a theological ghetto but who ventures forth for dialogue with many branches of human enquiry, sustained by his conviction of the unity of knowledge, a conviction that is underwritten by the oneness of the Creator, understood as the all-determining reality.

Finally, it is instructive to make a brief comparison of Pannenberg with another great twentieth-century theologian, equally strongly convinced of the unity of knowledge, Bernard Lonergan. His thought is formed by the Thomist tradition's belief that the search for understanding, if pursued through and through with an honest openness to discovery, will in the end prove to be the search for God, 'the unrestricted act of understanding'.[36] Lonergan's thinking is primarily philosophical and metaphysical, rather than biblical. He lauds the epistemological virtues of 'alertness, intelligence, reasonableness and responsibility,'[37] but he pays little attention to the specifics of the New Testament (Jesus Christ does not appear in the index of Lonergan's great book, *Insight*). Scien-

35. Albright and Haugen, *Beginning*, 438; cf. Polkinghorne, *Belief/Faith*, ch.9.
36. B. Lonergan, *Insight* (Longman, 1958), 684.
37. B. Lonergan, *Method in Theology* (Darton, Longman and Todd, 1973), 14.

tifically, he is principally concerned with the kinematic generalities of space and time, rather than the specific dynamic content of physical theory. When he does discuss physics, Lonergan displays a degree of technical facility, deriving from his competence in mathematics. (One might even suspect a slight degree of showing-off in the way he writes out equations in *Insight*.) There is the same recognition that we found in Pannenberg, that theology and the natural sciences have things to say to each other, together with a comparable reserve about engaging with specifics. Concern with scientific detail is to be found to a much greater degree in the writings of the scientist-theologians [38], but coupled in our case with much less theological sophistication. All these writers are making exploratory trips into the border region between theology and the natural sciences, not surprisingly mapping most accurately the territory that is nearest to their home base. Much still remains to be discovered in that fertile region.

8.2 THOMAS TORRANCE'S ENGAGEMENT WITH THE NATURAL SCIENCES

Thomas Torrance is a distinguished systematic theologian who writes from within the reformed tradition. He and Pannenberg are leaders among contemporary theologians who take the greatest interest in what the natural sciences have to say. It is instructive to see where they agree and where their approaches differ.

Both share the conviction that knowledge is one and that this unity is underwritten by the Oneness of God. Torrance

---

38. See Polkinghorne, *Scientists*.

repudiates the idea of life in the theological ghetto when he writes about theology that 'because it operates in the same world as natural science it cannot pursue its activity in a sealed-off enclave of its own'.[39] This emphasis on the unified character of human enquiry into reality carries with it the implication that the quest is also incomplete if it does not include theological investigation within its scope. One reason for this is that theology is needed to address those metaquestions that arise when the search for rational understanding is carried through without limit. Torrance tells us that the sciences other than theology 'are not ultimately self-explanatory, refraining from asking the question as to the ultimate rational ground that lies behind every field of knowledge'.[40] For Torrance, that ultimate ground is, of course, God.

Torrance is more explicitly detailed than Pannenberg in following through this indispensable necessity of taking the natural sciences seriously as part of the single quest for understanding. He makes much more appeal to the content of of science, concentrating on the physical sciences and saying comparatively little about the biological sciences and even less about the social sciences, which are such an important concern for Pannenberg. Torrance's scientific heroes are Faraday, Maxwell and Einstein, and it is from the development of classical field theory that he draws his greatest scientific inspiration. Once again we encounter the mistaken notion that fields are, somehow, in themselves a source of openness to the future. 'Already deep in the nineteenth century, especially with Faraday and Maxwell, there was a growing reali-

39. T. F. Torrance, *Space, Time and Incarnation* (Oxford University Press, 1969), viii.
40. T. F. Torrance, *God and Rationality* (Oxford University Press, 1971), 95.

sation that to understand the nature of the universe a rather different concept of order was needed to replace that of a necessary and mechanical order'.[41] Concerning Einstein's work, Torrance says, 'There now emerged the concept of a continuous field of space-time which interacts with the constituent matter/energy of the universe, integrating everything within it in accordance with its unitary yet variable objective rational order of *non-causal connections*'[42] (my italics). Non-causality was not what Einstein introduced, or would have wanted to, because he believed that our trust in the reality of the physical world required for its basis that the world should possess a determinate order—hence his opposition to modern quantum theory. Einstein's insistence on a realist interpretation of physics (which unfortunately he mistakenly identified with a belief in the naive objectivity of the physical world) is undoubtedly one of the reasons why he appeals so much to Torrance, a resolute realist in his understanding of theology.

Torrance frequently quotes Einstein's dictum that the universe is 'finite but unbounded', treating this as if it were a statement of the causal openness of cosmic process. However, the unboundedness being referred to is purely geometrical, comparable to the fact that the surface area of a sphere is finite but there is no natural boundary constituting the frontier of that finitude. If we are to find true openness in the physical world, the places to look for it would seem to be the domains of quantum theory, chaos theory and complexity theory. Torrance sometimes refers to quantum me-

41. A. R. Peacocke (ed.), *The Sciences and Theology in the Twentieth Century* (Oriel Press, 1981), 91.

42. T. F. Torrance, *Divine and Contingent Order* (Oxford University Press, 1981), 77–78.

chanics, and to the work of Ilya Prigogine on the spontaneous generation of large-scale order in dissipative systems,[43] but he does not make much of these ideas which could, in fact, be of fundamental significance for what he wants to achieve.[44] No one could question the greatness of his three scientific heroes, but they have had successors whose insights should also be taken into account.

Often Torrance seems to make metaphorical use of scientific categories in a way that seems insufficiently controlled by their actual meaning. It is difficult for a rather literal-minded physicist to know what is being asserted in a passage in which it is said that Jesus Christ

> forms a moving and creative centre for the confluence of world-lines from the pleroma of space-time. The movement of eternity into time in Jesus Christ has the effect of temporalizing space and spatializing time in an orderly succession of successive patterns of change and coherent structures within which God may reflect and fulfil His own creative and redemptive intentionality.[45]

Yet Torrance has made at least one brilliant use of a metaphorical resource drawn from science. This occurs in the comparison he makes between, on the one hand, the relationship of natural theology to revealed theology and, on the other hand, the relationship of geometry to physics.[46] Before Ein-

43. See I. Prigogine and I. Stengers, *Order out of Chaos* (Heinemann, 1984).
44. See Polkinghorne, *Belief in God*, ch. 3.
45. Torrance, *Incarnation*, 72.
46. T. F. Torrance, *Reality and Scientific Theology* (Scottish Academic Press, 1985), ch. 2.

stein, physics and geometry were considered to be distinct, with geometry defining the static structure of the spatial 'container' within which the independent dynamical interactions of physics then took place. The general theory of relativity changed all that, for it presents us with a single account in which matter curves space and space curves the paths of matter, so that geometry and physics are in intimate and integrated mutual relationship. In a very similar way, natural theology was traditionally presented as the prologue to revealed theology, the discussion of '*De Deo Uno*' setting the scene for the subsequent discussion of '*De Deo Trino*', the latter conducted in the light of Christian revelation. Torrance is surely right to insist, on the contrary, on the need for an integrated theological discourse. In isolation from revealed theology, natural theology too easily subsides into a deistic natural philosophy, which in turn will tend to sink further into pure naturalism. In isolation from natural theology, revealed theology loses an important point of contact with general human experience and then it too easily subsides into becoming an ecclesiastical language game.

Torrance's affirmation of an appropriate place for natural theology makes an important contribution to the development of theological thinking in the Reformed tradition. Torrance is recognised as a leading exponent and developer of the thought of the great Swiss Reformed theologian Karl Barth. Notoriously, Barth took a highly critical attitude towards attempts at natural theology. Torrance has succeeded in showing how revelation mediated through creation can be integrated with revelation uttered by God's Word in Jesus Christ. Much as Torrance admires Barth, he criticises him for a marked reluctance to engage with the insights of science.

However, what Karl Barth did not seem to appreciate adequately, was the fact that since God makes himself known to us in the created universe where he has placed us and therefore in and through the spatio-temporal structures and intelligibilities of the universe which, under God, are more and more disclosed to our scientific enquiries, there are basic interconnections between theological concepts and natural scientific concepts which have to be brought to light, if we are to do justice both to our knowledge of God and to our knowledge of the created order'.[47]

Although Torrance's detailed use of scientific ideas is not always immune from criticism by professional scientists, his efforts in this respect derive from no superficial desire to appear 'up to date' in a scientific age. Instead his engagement with science arises from his deep conviction that the character of our times is indeed stamped by the success of the natural sciences and that this provides a challenge to theology that the latter should welcome and can respond to in a positive and creative way. He tells us that 'whether we like it or not the whole of the future will be dominated by empirical science and anything that fails to stand up to its rigorous discipline will fall away'.[48] Hence the need for 'Theological Science', the title of one of Torrance's most important books.[49] Torrance shares with Pannenberg the concept of theology as the science of God. The influence of Karl Barth on his thinking ensures

47. T. F. Torrance, *Transformation and Convergence in the Frame of Knowledge* (Christian Journals, 1984), x.

48. Torrance, *Rationality*, 51.

49. T. F. Torrance, *Theological Science* (Oxford University Press, 1969).

that this understanding is differentiated sharply in his mind from any notion of theology as the science of religion. The self-revealing reality of God, and not the culturally influenced religious structures of human communities, is the true subject of theological concern. While it is true that 'the more scientifically we can pursue our theology, the more we shall be able to march forward as one, and the more relevant our message will be to a world which will always be dominated by empirical and theoretical science',[50] Torrance would agree with Pannenberg in a stout defence of the autonomy of theological thinking within its own proper domain. A strategy of assimilating science and theology to each other must be resisted for 'we cannot bring in from natural science 'evidence' to help us out of some point of theological difficulty'.[51]

As I have already indicated, contingency is as important a theme for Torrance as it is for Pannenberg. He affirms the ontological dependence of creation on the sustaining will of the Creator for its continuing existence, together with the openness of history towards the future. A third aspect of the universe's contingency is also important in Torrance's thought: the freely chosen character of the order which the divine will has bestowed upon the creation. Einstein once said that he was interested in what degree of choice the Lord had in fixing the laws of nature and the resulting form of the universe. Torrance believes that choice to have been wide, so that we as scientists have to look and see what God has actually selected. 'The intelligibility of the universe provides science with its confidence, but the contingency of the universe pro-

50. Torrance, *Incarnation*, ix.
51. Torrance, *Rationality*, 79.

vides science with its challenge'.[52] With the gift to creation of its fruitful order came also the divine gift of 'a contingent freedom of its own, grounded in the transcendent freedom of God and maintained through His free interaction with the universe'.[53] What we have called the kenotic character of the act of creation is expressed by Torrance when he writes, 'The creation of the universe as an autonomous reality distinct from God while dependent on Him also, involves the endowment of the universe with autonomous structures of its own'.[54]

When discussing these themes, Torrance presents us with a complex and nuanced account of the processes of creation in which order and contingency are intertwined and where these processes are open to God's interaction with their unfolding history. 'It is in this astonishing combination of unpredictability and lawfulness, not only in the history of man but in the history of all created reality in its relation to the constancy and freedom of the grace of the Creator, that lies behind the Christian conception of the cosmos as an open-ended universe'.[55] A scientist reading those words cannot help thinking of how well they resonate with our growing understanding of the way in which complex systems spontaneously generate order 'at the edge of chaos', [56] that is to say, in a region where order and disorder, predictability and unpredictability, intertwine, so that the system is neither so rigid that nothing new can ever happen, nor so loose that nothing coming into being can ever persist.

52. Torrance, *Divine and Contingent Order*, 58.
53. Ibid., 4.
54. Ibid., 37.
55. Ibid., 69.
56. See Kauffman, *Origins of Order*.

Three distinctive and particular themes characterise much of Torrance's thinking that is relevant to theology's interface with the natural sciences:

(i) *Epistemic conformity*. An insistent concern of Torrance's is that we should recognise that there is no universal epistemology, so that entities can only be known in a manner that conforms to the way that they actually are. 'You know something only in accordance with its nature, and you develop your knowledge of it as you allow its nature to prescribe for you the mode of rationality appropriate to it'.[57] As I have written elsewhere, there is an unavoidable (and benign) 'epistemic circle': 'how we know is controlled by the nature of the object and the nature of the object is revealed through our knowledge of it'.[58] A reflective scientist instantly recognises the justness of this claim. We know the macroscopic world of classical physics in one way, but the microscopic world of quantum theory is known in a quite different way that respects its Heisenbergian uncertainty. There is to be no undue tyranny of common-sense, no reduction of everything to an epistemological lowest common denominator. When we enter a new physical regime, we must be open to the possible revision of our ways of thinking and knowing. Rightly rejecting a view that scientists are perpetual sceptics, Torrance says, 'What [the scientist] does subject to doubt is his own assumptions about the object, and so he allows attachment to the object to help him detach himself from his own presuppositions'.[59]

57. Torrance, *Rationality*, 52.
58. Polkinghorne, *Belief/Faith*, 32.
59. Torrance, *Rationality*, 9.

The relevance of this to theology's search for knowledge of God is obvious:

> We cannot begin by forming independently a theory of how God is knowable and then seek to test it out or indeed actualise it and fill it with material content. How God can be known must be determined from first to last by the way in which He is actually known.[60]

Here is an extremely valuable contribution to our thinking which accords well with experience gained in science's own quest for understanding.

(ii) *Relational space.* We have already noted that relativity theory integrated geometry and physics, space and matter. Although the theory retained some absolutes (the speed of light, the space-time measure called proper time), it replaced the old container view of space, dominant from the Greeks to Newton, with a relational concept of space and time (judgements of simultaneity are relative to observers, moving bodies contract, moving clocks run slow). This emphasis on the relational character of reality was reinforced by quantum theory (interrelationship of observer and observed; the togetherness-in-separation, EPR effect, of quantum entities) and by chaos theory (exquisitely sensitive systems can never be isolated from the effects of their environment). Modern physics has repudiated the disjoint picture of atoms and the void in favour of a much more correlated account of reality.

Torrance attaches considerable theological significance to this relational point of view, which he believes is fully consonant with the thinking of the Nicene Fathers of the

---

60. Torrance, *Theological Science*, 9.

early Church.[61] When God was thought of as being outside the container of created space, the consequent separation between Creator and creation was too sharp to allow an adequate concept of divine incarnation. Even greater difficulty ensued when Newton identified his absolute space with the *sensorium* of God, for that made divine participation within that space a nonsensical contradiction. Torrance believes that this is what drove Newton to Arianism.[62] Only a concept of the universe as relational and dynamic can afford, in his view, a picture of creation consonant with a true divine incarnation within its history, for that requires 'a concept of space in terms of ontological and dynamic relationship between God and the physical universe'.[63] Torrance also shrewdly suggests that a container view of space encouraged an unduly reified kind of sacramentalism for, under its influence in the Western Church, 'supernatural grace was widely thought of as contained in ecclesiastical vessels and capable of being handed on in space and time by means of them'.[64]

(iii) *Incarnation.* Absolutely central to Torrance's thought is the full affirmation, in Chalcedonian terms, of the reality of the Incarnation, the historic event of the Word made flesh in Jesus Christ. Such an affirmation is welcome,[65] though some writers of science and theology have expressed a preference for formulating Christology in inspirational or functional terms.[66] Torrance finds in the Incarnation the focal point of Creator-creation interaction, in both directions.

61. Torrance, *Incarnation*, ch. 1.
62. Ibid., 39–40.
63. Ibid., 18.
64. Ibid., 25.
65. See Polkinghorne, *Belief/Faith*, ch. 7.
66. See Polkinghorne, *Scientists*, ch. 6.

The world then is made open to God through its intersection by the axis of Creation-Incarnation. Its space-
time structures are so organized in relation to God that
we who are set within them may think in and through
them to their transcendent ground in God Himself.
Jesus Christ constitutes the actual centre in space and
time where this may be done. But what of the same relationship the other way round, in the *openness of God*
for the world He has made? Does the intersection of
His reality with our this-worldly reality in Jesus Christ
mean anything for God? We have noted already that it
means that space and time are affirmed as real for God
in the actuality of His relationship with us, which binds
us to space and time, so that neither we nor God can
contract out of them. Does this not mean that God has
so opened Himself to our world that our this-worldly
experiences have import for Him in such a way, for example, that we must think of Him as taking our hurt
and pain into Himself?[67]

Two very important qualifications of classical theism's rather
austere account of God are given in that quotation. One is the
acknowledgement that, although God is, of course, eternal,
there is also a real divine relationship to the created reality of
time. Many writers in the field of science and theology have
wished also to affirm this, but they have often done so by bor-
rowing from process theology the concept of a polarity of the
eternal and the temporal within the divine nature.[68] Torrance's

---

67. Torrance, *Incarnation*, 74.
68. See Polkinghorne, *Scientists*, 41; K. Ward, *Rational Theology and the Creativity of God* (Blackwell, 1982); and chapter 7 in this volume.

approach is differently grounded because of its direct appeal to the Incarnation, the appearance of the Eternal within time. It is certainly difficult to see how the religion of the Incarnate Christ could not take divine involvement with time with the utmost seriousness.

The second qualification relates to classical theism's account of divine impassibility, which led Thomas Aquinas to say that though God acts on creation, creation does not act on God. Of course, there could be no notion of creatures being able magically to manipulate God, but so extreme an expression of divine invulnerability is hard to reconcile with the insight that God is love. Torrance believes that the implication drawn from the Incarnation of a divine participation in creation's travail is further reinforced by the fact that our knowledge of the dynamical contingency of the world has freed us from the medieval trap of entertaining 'notions of the impassibility and immutability of God which had as their counterpart a notion of the world which, given its initial momentum by the First Cause, constituted a system of necessary and causal relations in which it was very difficult to find room for any genuine contingence'.[69]

Among leading contemporary theologians, Thomas Torrance displays the greatest concern to integrate into theological thinking insights that can legitimately be derived from the natural sciences. Details of how this is done can sometimes be criticised by scientists themselves, but they should also display admiration and gratitude for the whole-hearted way in which the enterprise has been undertaken.

69. Torrance, *Rationality*, 6.

8.3 PAUL DAVIES' ENGAGEMENT WITH THEOLOGY

Paul Davies is a theoretical physicist who is also a very successful popular writer about science. His many books are characterised by clear expositions of quite detailed and deep scientific ideas and by a well-conveyed air of excitement about
the advance of knowledge. Part of the secret of his success is
that he has a journalistic capacity to identify and tell a good
story. At times this leads him to transgress one of the rules
for the scrupulous popular expositor: make absolutely clear
which ideas are widely accepted in the scientific community
and which are still the subject of conjecture and continuing
debate. For example, in his book on quantum theory, *Other
Worlds*,[70] there is insufficient acknowledgement of the highly
contentious character of the many-worlds interpretation of
quantum mechanics.

In 1983, Davies' writing took a new turn with the publication of *God and the New Physics*, with its by now notorious claim
that 'it may seem bizarre, but in my opinion science offers a
surer path to God than religion'.[71] Here was a kind of natural theology being practised, not by pious scientists who were
adherents of a faith tradition, but by a free-standing enquirer
who sensed that there was more to be told about the story
of the universe than had met the unaided scientific eye alone.
This was followed in 1992 by *The Mind of God*, a 'more considered attempt,'[72] whose title capitalised on the way in which
Stephen Hawking had flirted with theistic language in *A Brief*

70. P. Davies, *Other Worlds* (Dent, 1980).
71. P. Davies, *God and the New Physics* (Dent, 1983), ix.
72. P. Davies, *The Mind of God* (Simon and Schuster, 1992), 14.

History of Time,[73] where God appears frequently in the text but does not figure in the index. By 1995, Davies had been awarded the Templeton Prize for Progress in Religion.

These developments are striking because Davies does not at all entertain a modest conception of the role of scientific understanding. We are told that 'fundamental physics is pointing the way to a new appreciation of man and of his place in the universe'[74] and that 'a unified description of all creation could be within our [scientific] grasp'.[75] About a highly speculative idea concerning the very early universe, Davies claims that 'the implications of the Hartle-Hawking universe for theology are profound,'[76] despite the judgement of theologians that questions of temporal origin are not at all central to the doctrine of creation, which focuses on the answer to the ontological question of why the world exists at all.

When we examine the arguments that persuade Davies to look beyond science in the search for a deeper and more comprehensive understanding, we find that they are precisely those which have been the basis for the revived and revised natural theology also advocated by more conventionally religious scientists.[77] The deep intelligibility and rational beauty of the physical world are encouragements to a belief that there is an Intelligence behind its pattern and structure. The fine-tuning of the laws of physics, which was indispensable for the possibility of the evolution of carbon-based life, encourages

73. S. W. Hawking, *A Brief History of Time* (Bantam, 1988).
74. Davies, *God and the New Physics*, vii.
75. Ibid., vii.
76. Davies, *Mind of God*, 68.
77. See J. C. Polkinghorne, *Science and Creation* (SPCK, 1988), chs. 1 and 2; *Scientists*, ch. 4.

the thought that there is a Purpose to be discerned at work in cosmic history. Two particular themes recur with emphasis in Davies' thinking:

(i) *The Laws of Nature*. Davies asks the question, Where do physical laws come from? He is not content to take them, in their orderly fruitfulness, as unexplained brute fact. Davies tells us, 'Personally I feel more comfortable with a deeper level of explanation than the laws of physics. Whether the use of the term "God" for that deeper level is appropriate is, of course, a matter of debate'.[78] He does not wish to follow David Hume's advice to treat matter and its properties simply as given brute fact. When considering the alternatives of a necessary world or a necessary being as providing the basis to be assumed as the ground of subsequent explanation, Davies is able to say, 'In my own mind I have no doubts at all that the arguments for a necessary world are far shakier than the arguments for a necessary being, so my personal inclination is to opt for the latter'. Yet he immediately goes on to say that it is not 'obvious to me that this postulated being who underpins the rationality of the world has much relationship to the personal God of religion, still less to the God of the bible or the Koran'.[79] This is a point to which we shall return.

(ii) *Consciousness*. The second theme to which Davies attaches great significance is the emergence of consciousness in the course of cosmic history. For many of us, the most remarkable event following the big bang, of which we have knowledge, has been the universe's becoming aware of itself through humanity—the event that, among other consequences, has

78. Davies, *Mind of God*, 189.
79. Ibid., 191.

made science possible. Davies tells us that he has 'come to the point of view that mind—i.e. conscious awareness of the world—is not a meaningless and accidental quirk of nature, but an absolutely fundamental fact of reality'.[80] While biologists, as part of their stubborn refusal to accept any concept of progress through evolution, often seem to regard the mental as just another survival trick (without being able to explain convincingly why *awareness*, as opposed to the capacity for information processing, has this character), many physicists are not at all readily disposed to take this dismissive view. In *The Mind of God*, Davies devotes a lot of space to discussing the nature of mathematics. He does not commit himself to a definite answer, but many mathematicians believe that their subject is concerned with discovery and not mere construction, so that there is a noetic world of mathematical truths which we are privileged to explore and which, in Davies' phrase, is 'out there'.[81]

We have already noted that Paul Davies is distinguished from many other writers on these topics because of his complete detachment from any religious tradition. This produces a considerable degree of limitation in his engagement with theology which, though far from exhibiting the kind of naivety of which it is easy to convict a writer such as Stephen Hawking, is nevertheless kept within unsatisfactorily narrow bounds. In *God and the New Physics*, Davies tells us that he has 'made no attempt to discuss religious experience or questions of morality'.[82] That, of course, is his choice but it makes it

80. Ibid., 16; cf. P. Davies, *The Fifth Miracle* (Penguin Press, 1998).
81. Ibid., 141; cf. Polkinghorne, *Belief in God*, ch. 6.
82. Davies, *God and the New Physics*, viii.

scarcely surprising that he does not discover a God 'who bears much relation to the personal God of religion, still less the God of the bible or the Koran'. He has not been looking in the right place.

Davies has a fideistic understanding of religion and he shows little recognition of the nature of theology as a rational enquiry based on a search for understanding derived from motivated belief.[83] Statements such as 'the world's major religions, founded on received wisdom and dogma, are rooted in the past and do not cope easily with changing times',[84] and 'the true believer must stand by his faith whatever the apparent evidence against it' [85] present an obscurantist and irrational account of religious thinking which I repudiate. There is no recognition of theology as being, in Anselm's famous phrase, 'faith seeking understanding'.

In his writing, Davies occasionally presents the discussion of an argument in the form of a dialogue. On these occasions, the spokesperson for conventional religion is as naive and unconvincing as is Simplicio, the defender of the Ptolemaic system in Galileo's famous *Dialogue Concerning the Two Chief World Systems*. When 'Believer' starts a discussion by saying, 'in my opinion, miracles are the best proof that God exists',[86] he is setting off on the wrong foot. Such arguments may have played a part in a pre-critical age (one thinks of Pascal in the *Pensées*), but no theologian today would take so bald an approach to the issue. Of course, Christian theology cannot evade the question of miracle, because of the central sig-

---

83. Cf. Polkinghorne, *Scientists*, ch. 2.
84. Davies, *God and the New Physics*, 2.
85. Ibid., 6.
86. Ibid., 191.

nificance of its claim of Christ's resurrection, but its account would be much more careful and nuanced.[87] Davies' discussion is made further unsatisfactory by its concentrating on levitation and walking on water, with a complete neglect of the resurrection. For the theist, the critical question in relation to the miraculous is that of divine consistency (such events, if they are to be *theologically* credible, must be capable of being understood as signs of a deeper insight into God's relation to creation, and not as mere tours de force). That is why a Christian consideration of the issue must start with the resurrection and not with less significant, and so more questionable, wonders.

In so far as Davies makes reference to theologians, it is usually to people like Augustine or Aquinas whose writings combine theology with philosophy, with the quotations chosen from the philosophical side of their concerns. In fact, both of these great thinkers would regret an unbalanced engagement with their thought, which they would conceive to be of a truth-seeking unity. It is a quaint feature of Davies' writing that when he refers to contemporary theologians, such a Thomas Torrance, he habitually calls them 'philosophers'.

Another feature, perhaps more irritating than quaint, is that Davies virtually never refers to people of similar scientific background to himself who are also Christian believers and theologically aware, such as the scientist-theologians Ian Barbour, Arthur Peacocke and myself.[88] We appear to be natural conversation partners, but this particular engagement has been declined. Perhaps that is because Davies seems to be

---

87. Cf. J. C. Polkinghorne, *Science and Providence* (SPCK, 1989), ch. 4.
88. See Polkinghorne, *Scientists*, for a summary of our approaches.

under the misapprehension that religion belongs to 'a bye-gone age'.[89]

Davies tells us that he belongs 'to the group of scientists who do not subscribe to conventional religion but nevertheless deny that the universe is a purposeless accident'.[90] At the end of his first book, this led him to the notion of 'a natural rather than a supernatural God',[91] a kind of super-intelligent demiurge who had contrived much of the order and fruitfulness that science discerns since, in Davies' opinion, 'it is perfectly possible for much, if not all, of what we encounter in the universe to be the product of intelligent manipulation of a purely natural kind'.[92] All this would, of course, have to be attained within the framework of the laws of physics which, from this point of view, retain the mystery of their given character. Davies acknowledged that 'physics can, perhaps, explain the content, origin and organization of the physical universe, but not the laws (or superlaw) of physics itself'.[93] A substantial unexplained mystery remained.

This early account neatly illustrated one of the classical criticisms of unaided natural theology: that the finite evidence to which it appeals can never establish the existence of an *infinite* Being. The best that could be done in that respect would be to follow those who, like Richard Swinburne,[94] argue that an infinite God is a simpler concept than a finite demiurge.

In his second, 'more considered', volume, the discussion is more refined. Davies looks at the neoplatonic ideas of John

89. Davies, *Fifth Miracle*, 203.
90. Davies, *Mind of God*, 16.
91. Davies, *God and the New Physics*, 209.
92. Ibid., 208.
93. Ibid., 216.
94. R. Swinburne, *Is There a God?* (Oxford University Press, 1996), ch. 3.

Leslie,[95] who suggests that 'ethical requirement' could bring the universe into being. Davies comments,

> My own inclination is to suppose that qualities such as ingenuity, economy, beauty and so on have a genuine transcendent reality—they are not merely the products of human experience—and that these qualities are reflected in the structure of the natural world. Whether such qualities can themselves bring the universe into existence I don't know.[96]

Such caution is wise. I have suggested that Leslie's view is an attempt to turn the axiological argument for the existence of God into a free-standing principle of ontology, a burden that it cannot sustain.[97]

In a rare moment of engagement with a specific kind of theology, Davies expresses himself as being 'closely in tune with process thought', [98] though this seems more to be in relation to the general idea of a divine guidance of cosmic process within the grain of physical law than an endorsement of A. N. Whitehead's event-dominated metaphysics (whose relationship to quantum physics is much more problematic than Davies seems to recognise [99]). *The Mind of God* ends with a statement of Davies' credo:

> I cannot believe that our existence in this universe is a mere quirk of fate, an incidental blip in the great cosmic drama. Our involvement is too intimate. The physical species *Homo* may count for nothing, but the

95. J. Leslie, *Value and Existence* (Blackwell, 1979).
96. Davies, *Mind of God*, 14.
97. Polkinghorne, *Belief/Faith*, 58.
98. Davies, *Mind of God*, 192.
99. Polkinghorne, *Belief in God*, 55–56.

existence of mind in some organism on some planet in the universe is surely a fact of fundamental significance. Through conscious beings the universe has generated self-awareness. This can be no trivial detail, no minor byproduct of mindless, purposeless forces. We are truly meant to be here. [100]

Paul Davies' significance for theology is primarily as an exemplar. In this way he illustrates two facts about natural theology. The first is that it is a feasible rational enterprise in the modern world, conducted in the modest mode of an insightful enquiry into limit questions that arise from science but go beyond the latter's circumscribed field of investigation. The theistic answers suggested are not logically coercive but they are plausible and intellectually satisfying, even to someone who brings to them no prior inclination to espouse such belief. To see that this is so is an encouragement to those of us who, from within a religious tradition, make use of similar insights. It is clear that we are not just allowing the wish to be father to the thought.

The second fact about natural theology illustrated in Davies' writings is its insubstantiality when unallied with insights drawn from wider experience, including the encounter with the sacred, preserved and propagated in the world faith traditions. Interesting, and indeed moving, as are some of Davies' thoughts on the significance of the universe and its history, there is a theological thinness about them which substantiates Torrance's insistence that natural and revealed theology belong together and that neither can satisfactorily be pursued in isolation.

100. Davies, *Mind of God*, 232.

CHAPTER NINE

Science and Theology in England

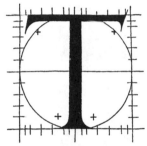 HIS brief historical survey restricts it-
self to England. An account of the
same subject in relation to Scotland
would be somewhat different, and one
in relation to North America much
more so. Some of the differences stem
from contrasting national characters.
The Scots have always manifested a more overtly intellectually
serious attitude towards life than the English. (The traditional
Scottish respect for the Dominie, the local schoolmaster, was
not quite paralleled in England.) Systematic theology has
been an enduring Scottish academic interest. Academy in
North America has been heir to a great variety of influences,
with the Continental European at least as significant as the
British. Other differences stem from the particular role that
the Church of England has played in English national life.
Anglicanism has always sought to found its theological thinking on the triple basis of scripture, tradition and reason. It attaches importance to an easy dialogue with secular learning,

an emphasis that could not fail to be consolidated by the monopoly held by the Church of England over the two ancient universities of Oxford and Cambridge until late in the nineteenth century. The strengths of English theological scholarship have tended to lie in biblical and patristic studies rather than in systematic theology. Its feeder discipline has traditionally been classics and not philosophy.

A byproduct of this emphasis on sound learning has been the long English history of interaction between theology and science. The interchange has never been a major activity but it has been a persistent one. It was adumbrated in the Middle Ages with Robert Grosseteste's concern with light, both as a physical phenomenon and as a spiritual symbol. The metaphysical scheme of his treatise *De Luce* considers light as the subtle prime matter of creation from which all else developed according to immanent principles.

A common theme in seventeenth-century English thinking was that of the 'two books' that God had written: the book of nature and the book of scripture. We find this idea, relating the insights of a nascent science to the traditional insights of theology, expressed in that century in the writings of Francis Bacon, Sir Thomas Browne and Robert Boyle. Natural theology always had a strong appeal to the English, particularly in the form of 'physico-theology', appealing to the aptness of living beings and the regularity of the world in order to establish the credibility of belief in a divine Designer. From John Ray's *Wisdom of God Manifested in the Works of Creation* (1691) through William Paley's celebrated *Natural Theology* (1802) and on to the Bridgewater Treatises (1833–36) concerned with 'The Power, Wisdom and Goodness of God as manifested in the Creation', the English were uninhibited in their commitment to this form of the Argument from Design. Only the alternative insights of Darwin (1859) could bring the pursuit of this particular kind of natural theology to a sudden halt.

Later in the nineteenth century, F. J. A. Hort not only edited the Greek text of the New Testament with B. F. Westcott but he also examined in the Natural Sciences Tripos in Cambridge. Hort was a man who published much less than he thought or knew, but in his Hulsean Lectures, *The Way, the Truth and the Life*, he wrote that 'if it was necessary that man should come to know God above, it was also necessary that he should come to know the world below' and he went on to welcome the fact that, through science, there is now 'added a knowledge of the constituent elements and forces of the world, and of its history in the past'.[1] The Anglicans Charles Kingsley, Aubrey Moore and Frederick Temple all played important parts in welcoming the insights of Charles Darwin, perceiving that an evolutionary world can be understood theologically as a creation allowed by its Creator 'to make itself'. Moore wrote in *Lux Mundi* (1889) that 'science has pushed the deist's God further and further away, and at the moment when it seemed as if He would be thrust out all together, Darwinism appeared, and, under the guise of a foe, did the work of a friend'.[2] In other words, an occasionally interventionist God had been removed from the agenda, to the greater health of theology. Either God was at work, everywhere and at all times, through the unfolding processes of creation, or God was absent from the world altogether. Twentieth-century writers such as Arthur Peacocke, and in

1. F. J. A. Hort, *The Way, the Truth and the Life* (Macmillan, 1893), 80–81.
2. Quoted by A. R. Peacocke in J. Durant (ed.), *Darwinism and Divinity* (Oxford University Press, 1985), 111.

the United States Ian Barbour, would later continue this theme and develop it under the rubric of divine *creatio continua*.[3] Creation is no longer to be thought of as a once for all decree, but as an unfolding process.

One may also note that in the nineteenth century, which is so often seen as a time of conflict between science and religion, the great British physicists of the day, Faraday, Maxwell, Kelvin and Stokes, were all men of deep religious faith. James Clerk Maxwell's deep insight and formidable mathematical powers enabled him to discover the unified theory of electricity and magnetism, an achievement comparable to Newton's discovery of universal gravitation. Maxwell was the first Cavendish Professor of Physics at Cambridge and he caused to have inscribed in Latin over the archway leading to the Cavendish Laboratory the verse from Psalm III, 'Great are the works of the Lord, studied by all who have pleasure in them'.

This interaction between science and theology has continued in the twentieth century. Between the wars, the distinguished astrophysicist Sir Arthur Eddington, and his scientific sparring partner Sir James Jeans, both expressed in their highly successful popular writings a feeling that developments in our understanding of the history of the universe and the nature of physical process were congenial to taking seriously a spiritual dimension to reality. Eddington was responsible for two influential images conveying the limited character of science. One was the figure of 'the two tables': the solid wooden object of common experience and the ghostly entity of scien-

3. I. G. Barbour, *Issues in Science and Religion* (SCM Press, 1966), ch. 12; A. R. Peacocke, *Creation and the World of Science* (Oxford University Press, 1979), ch. 2.

tific theory, mostly empty space but containing some quantum probability wave-patterns as well. He commented ironically, 'I need not tell you that modern physics has by delicate test and remorseless logic assured me that my second table is the only one that is really there—wherever "there" may be'.[4] A point is being made, but in a slightly cheap and polemical way. The other image was of the fisherman with a two-inch mesh to his net, who concludes that all fish are at least two inches long.[5] Here a more serious point is being made, for impersonal science does indeed trawl experience with a coarse-grained net. Eddington was a Quaker and his religious beliefs and experiences, which were clearly of great importance to him, are expressed in doctrinally unfocussed language. The word he liked to use was 'mysticism', meaning not the intense unitive experience of a St John of the Cross, but a more everyday consciousness of the sacred. Jeans, much more than Eddington, was deeply impressed by the role of beautiful mathematics as the key to unlock the secrets of the physical world. In his best-selling book *The Mysterious Universe* he wrote, 'the great Architect of the Universe now begins to appear as a pure mathematician'.[6] Both these distinguished scientists encouraged the recognition of the possibility of friendship between science and religion, but their occasional thoughts on the matter did not have sufficient theological depth to contribute much to the intellectual assessment of the encounter.

A philosophical theologian who took science very seri-

4. A. S. Eddington, *The Nature of the Physical World* (Cambridge University Press, 1928), xiv.

5. A. S. Eddington, *The Philosophy of Physical Science* (Cambridge University Press, 1949), 16.

6. J. Jeans, *The Mysterious Universe* (Cambridge University Press, 1930), 134.

ously was the now almost-forgotten F. R. Tennant. He maintained a version of the design argument but framed it in terms very different from those of Paley. Tennant looked to the intelligibility and general character of the physical world as providing grounds for belief in cosmic design. 'The forcibleness of Nature's suggestion that she is the outcome of intelligent design lies not in particular cases of adaptedness in the world, nor even in the multiplicity of these ... [but] consists rather in the conspiration of innumerable causes to produce, either by united or reciprocal action, and to maintain, a general order of nature'. These words, written in the 1930s, prefigure lines of thought that would be vigorously pursued by others more than forty years later. In describing this 'wider teleology',[7] Tennant is credited with coining the adjective 'anthropic', though doubtless it was independently recoined by the English astrophysicist Brandon Carter[8] when he made his seminal comments, inaugurating the modern-style discussion of Anthropic Principle coincidences. It was only with this latter, more focussed appeal to scientific insights that a revived and revised natural theology really got under weigh, an activity in which English contributors have played a significant role.

Charles Raven was Regius Professor of Divinity at Cambridge in the late 1940s and he was keenly interested in natural history. He maintained the English tradition of a positive theological evaluation of evolution, writing on this theme in terms more measured and less mystical than those employed by Teilhard de Chardin, thereby reflecting the modest, un-

7. F. R. Tennant, *Philosophical Theology*, vol. 2 (Cambridge University Press, 1930), 79.

8. B. Carter in M. S. Longair (ed.), *Confrontation of Cosmological Theories with Observation* (Reidel, 1974), 29.

rhetorical tone that has tended to characterise English discourse. The first volume of his Gifford Lectures[9] is devoted to a survey of theologically informed attitudes to nature from the times of the biblical writers onwards. Raven was particularly at home with the gently reasonable religion of the seventeenth-century Cambridge platonists (Benjamin Whichcote, Ralph Cudworth, Henry More and their followers). He deplored the increasingly mechanised picture of nature that had stemmed from the ideas of Descartes and Newton and he greeted with relief the twentieth-century demise of the merely mechanical, which Raven attributed to Einstein and (with much greater justice) to the discoverers of quantum theory.

The tradition of Christian thinking that takes its inspiration from St Thomas Aquinas has always been concerned to set theology within a wide and generous intellectual context. Eric Mascall, who had studied mathematics as a young man, was an English Thomist whose Bampton Lectures of 1956,[10] though inevitably now dated, represent one of the first attempts to treat the interaction of science and theology in a modern manner that seeks to do professional justice to both disciplines. One may note that Mascall took a decidedly reserved view of Tennant's wider teleology.

More recently, Arthur Peacocke and myself, both of us coming to theology after long professional research careers in science, have sought to further the interaction between the two disciplines.[11] We belong to a growing clan of what might

9. C. E. Raven, *Science and Religion* (Cambridge University Press, 1953).

10. E. L. Mascall, *Christian Theology and Natural Science* (Longmans, 1956).

11. For a survey and comparison of the work of Peacocke and myself, together with our American colleague Ian Barbour, see J. C. Polkinghorne, *Scientists as Theologians* (SPCK, 1996).

be called scientist-theologians. Today, the scene is also becoming more professionalised, with Fraser Watts, a psychologist, holding at Cambridge the first endowed post in Britain devoted to Theology and the Natural Sciences. In England and elsewhere, talented young people are beginning to enter the subject through participation in Ph.D. programmes.

In an interdisciplinary encounter of this kind it is natural to consider whether a ground for meeting, and an arbiter for settling differences, might not be found in philosophy. Here a striking difference becomes apparent between the English and Continental styles of thought. One feels that every German theologian writes with Kant looking over one shoulder and Hegel looking over the other. For good or ill, the English tend to enjoy a more relaxed relationship with philosophy. We do not feel that John Locke is looking over our shoulder, though we cannot be altogether oblivious of the quizzical scrutiny of that stout Scottish sceptic David Hume. In so far as the British empirical tradition in philosophy affects us, it is principally in the form of a general encouragement to seek to ground understanding in experience.

This tendency is particularly prevalent in the scientific community, among whom there is considerable reserve about the way in which the second-order commentaries of the philosophers of science relate to first-order experiences of actually doing science. The stance taken by reflective scientists is that of a critical realism. We have seen that, in essence, the defence of scientific realism is an empirical defence: this is the way things have been found to be. Critical realism is not a logical claim about what must be true in all possible worlds, but it is a specific claim about what has been found to be the case in our actual world. It seems that we live in a universe so constituted, and are ourselves persons so constituted, that science is possible.

Scientist-theologians like Peacocke and myself—and in North America, Barbour—have sought to defend an analogous critical realist approach to theology.[12] Of course, there are big differences between theology's concern with the One who transcends us and who can properly be encountered only with awe and obedience, and science's concern with a physical world that we transcend and can put to the experimental test. Nevertheless we feel that we discern a degree of cousinly relationship between the two disciplines in that both are committed to a search for truth (a truth never wholly attained but to some degree approximated to). This critical realist quest for the best explanation provides, in our view, a common ground on which the dialogue between science and theology can take place.

Such thinking encourages an approach to theology that I described in my Gifford Lectures as 'bottom-up thinking'.[13] It seeks to proceed from the basement of evidence and experience to the higher level of theological understanding, whilst acknowledging that, no more in theology than in science, can we escape the inevitable intertwining of event and interpretation. In both disciplines we have to believe in order to understand, as well as understanding in order that we may believe.

Bottom-up theology roots its Christian account in the economic Trinity (revelatory acts of the Triune God) and it does not aspire to speak of the essential Trinity (the divine nature in itself) other than through the Church's encounter

12. Ibid.
13. J. C. Polkinghorne, *Science and Christian Belief/The Faith of a Physicist* (SPCK/Princeton University Press, 1994).

with the economic Trinity. 'Rahner's Rule'—that the economic Trinity is the essential Trinity—can be understood as a statement of critical theological realism in this sense, a belief that such an approach from below will be trustworthy.

English people and scientists are both prone to be suspicious of grand general principles that are not experientially earthed, and so an English scientist is doubly inclined to this way of thinking. I do not claim that it is the only way to approach theology but I believe that it affords a distinctive theological perspective, comparable to the perspectives, say, of liberation theology or feminist theology. Every specific point of view contains potentialities both for benefit derived from its particular insight and for distortion deriving from the limitation of its particular perspective. Certainly, the bottom-up approach will be an appropriate apologetic strategy for Christian witness to the scientific community, but externally oriented apologetics can only have real effectiveness if they also correspond internally to faith's quest for understanding, pursued with scrupulosity.

We have seen that the English have always had an inclination towards natural theology and today we see a revival of natural theology in the English-speaking world. It is taking place more at the hands of the scientists (including some, like Paul Davies,[14] who stand outside any conventional religious tradition) than at the hands of the theologians proper. This new natural theology is also *revised*. It is modest in its ambition, claiming only intellectually satisfying insight rather than logical proof. In fact, in the twentieth century after Kurt

---

14. P. C. W. Davies, *God and the New Physics* (Dent, 1983); *The Mind of God* (Simon and Schuster, 1992).

Gödel, we have come to see that proof is a limited, and in some ways unsatisfactory, category. The new natural theology is no rival to science but it seeks to complement it. It does not purport to answer questions that rightly lie in science's domain (such as how life originated on Earth) but it looks to the ground of science's explanation and goes on to ask whether the laws of nature are sufficiently self-contained to afford a fundamental basis for understanding the world, or whether they do not point beyond themselves to a deeper Ground of explanation. This discussion revolves around two great meta-questions, arising from scientific experience but going beyond science's own self-limited power to answer: 'Why is science possible?' and 'Why is the universe so (anthropically) special?'.[15]

Natural theology and creation are commonplace issues for discussion between science and theology. Recently, however, there has been an increasing realisation that their mutual dialogue must also move on to embrace topics of yet more central significance for each discipline. During the 1990s in the English-speaking world, there has been considerable engagement with questions relating to divine action and how it may be conceived of in the light of science's account of the orderly process of the physical world. In this discussion, science must be prepared to reconsider its account of causality and theology its account of providence.

One might hope that a bridge between the two might be afforded by philosophy's offering a metaphysics which is humble enough to pay respect to the conditions that both sci-

---

15. See J. C. Polkinghorne, *Reason and Reality* (SPCK, 1991), ch. 6; *Belief in God in an Age of Science* (Yale University Press, 1998), ch. 1.

ence and theology would wish to impose upon it, but also bold enough to forge a chain of connection. The links in that chain will not be the tight links of logical entailment, but they will be alogical links of consonant relationship. Similar conditions of consonance will originate from the theological end.

The pragmatically minded English have made their own characteristic contributions to a dialogue between science and theology that has been continuing for centuries. We have no desire, however, to be Little Englanders and we recognise that this conversation is now world-wide and that it is increasingly drawing in all the great world faith traditions. Exciting times lie ahead for the international exploration of the relationship between the truths of science and the truth of God.

Index

Index